CW01390724

SNAPREVISE

SnapRevise Text Guide:
Wuthering Heights
by Emily Brontë

Nirvana Prasad

InStudent Education UK Ltd owner of SnapRevise® trademark.
43 Priston Close, Worle, BS22 7FL, Weston-Super-Mare, United Kingdom

www.snaprevise.co.uk

Copyright © InStudent Publishing Pty Ltd 2024

All rights reserved. These notes are protected by copyright owned by InStudent Publishing Pty Ltd and you may not reproduce, disseminate, or communicate to the public the whole or a substantial part thereof except as permitted at law or with the prior written consent of InStudent Publishing Pty Ltd.

Title: Wuthering Heights by Emily Brontë Text Guide
ISBN: 978-1-917424-52-3

Published by InStudent Education UK Ltd CN 15550989 under licence from InStudent Publishing Pty Ltd.
ACN 624 188101

Disclaimer

No reliance on warranty. These SnapRevise materials are intended to supplement but are not intended to replace or to be any substitute for your regular school attendance, for referring to prescribed texts, or for your own note taking. You are responsible for following the appropriate syllabus, attending school classes, and maintaining good study practices. It is your responsibility to evaluate the accuracy of any information, opinions, and advice in these materials. Under no circumstance will InStudent Publishing Pty Ltd or InStudent Education UK Ltd ("Publishers"), their officers, agents, or employees be liable for any loss or damage caused by your use or reliance on these materials, including any adverse impact upon your performance in any academic subject as a result of your use or reliance on the materials. You accept that all information provided or made available by the Publishers is in the nature of general information and does not constitute advice. It is not guaranteed to be error-free and you should always independently verify any information, including through use of a professional teacher and other reliable resources. To the extent permissible at law, the Publishers expressly disclaim all warranties or guarantees of any kind, whether express or implied, including without limitation any warranties concerning the accuracy or content of information provided in these materials or other fitness for purpose. The Publishers shall not be liable for any direct, indirect, special, incidental, consequential or punitive damages of any kind. You agree to indemnify the Publishers, its officers, agents, and employees against any loss whatsoever by using these materials.

Preface

My name is Nirvana and I graduated in 2022. Some people might say I dodged a bullet because I never had to study *Wuthering Heights* for school, but I think it would have been a pretty great story to discuss in class. I read this book when I was the 'strange' kid in year 8, and it sparked in me a lifelong fascination with the Gothic. Now, as a perfectly normal undergraduate student, I can safely say it was one of the best books I've ever read. I don't spend all day thinking about Byronic heroes and tragic romances anymore, but I'll always be ready to talk someone's ear off about this book.

Wuthering Heights might be an insanely convoluted tale of twisted families and characters who are all named after each other, but the raw emotion and passion that threads its way through the book makes it unforgettable (once you finally understand who is who, that is). So I hope that you'll give yourself the chance to truly appreciate this masterpiece!

— Nirvana Prasad

Contents

~ SnapRevise® ~

Section 1

Nutshell Summary

Character family tree

This is a diagram of the two main family trees featured in the story. As many characters have similar names in the story, let's differentiate them right from the start to avoid confusion. For the purposes of this Text Guide, I will mostly be referring to characters by their first names (as there are many Lintons and Earnshaws). The original Catherine, who falls in love with Heathcliff, will be known as Catherine, and her daughter will be Cathy.

A few important characters are not visible here as they are not a part of either family tree. These include Mr Lockwood, the narrator, who occupies Thrushcross Grange from 1801, and Ellen 'Nelly' Dean, the housekeeper who recounts the story of Heathcliff and Catherine to Lockwood. An honourable mention can be made for Joseph, the groundskeeper of Wuthering Heights who, like Nelly, is an almost permanent fixture on the property.

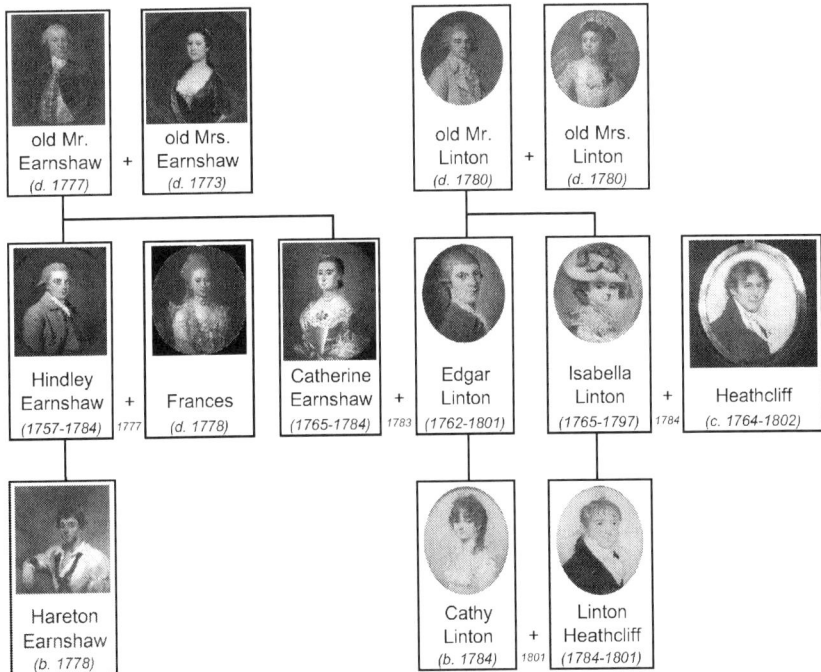

old Mr. Earnshaw (d. 1777) + old Mrs. Earnshaw (d. 1773)

old Mr. Linton (d. 1780) + old Mrs. Linton (d. 1780)

Hindley Earnshaw (1757-1784) + [1777] Frances (d. 1778)

Catherine Earnshaw (1765-1784) + [1783] Edgar Linton (1762-1801)

Isabella Linton (1765-1797) + [1784] Heathcliff (c. 1764-1802)

Hareton Earnshaw (b. 1778)

Cathy Linton (b. 1784) + [1801] Linton Heathcliff (1784-1801)

Source: shakko. Wikimedia Commons CC-BY-SA 3.0,
https://commons.wikimedia.org/wiki/File:Wuthering_Heights_family_tree.jpg

Summary

The story is narrated by Mr Lockwood, a new tenant at Thrushcross Grange. He goes to meet his landlord Heathcliff who lives at Wuthering Heights. Here, he also meets Cathy Heathcliff (**nee** Linton), the landlord's recently widowed daughter-in-law, and Hareton Earnshaw, an uneducated boy treated like a servant. Trapped in the house overnight due to a storm, he also meets the ghost of Catherine Earnshaw.

Curious about the residents of Wuthering Heights, Lockwood questions the housekeeper at Thrushcross Grange, Nelly. She tells a tragic story about the Earnshaw family who originally owned Wuthering Heights and the Linton family who originally owned Thrushcross Grange in recent decades. Presently, Heathcliff (who was raised by the Earnshaws) owns both estates and Nelly **regales** us with a tale of love, revenge, and obsession.

Wuthering Heights was originally the property of the Earnshaw family: Old Mr Earnshaw, his wife, and their two children, Hindley and Catherine. One day, following an extended trip, Old Mr Earnshaw returns with an orphaned boy who is named Heathcliff and adopted into the family. Heathcliff quickly befriends Catherine, whereas Hindley takes an immediate disliking to him.

Following the death of his father, Hindley becomes the master of the house and reduces Heathcliff's status to that of a servant, forbidding him from interacting with Catherine. However, the two children continue to play with each other against his wishes. One day, they sneak down to Thrushcross Grange, which then housed Old Mr Linton, his wife, and their two children, Edgar and Isabella.

While there, Catherine sustains an injury and is cared for by the Linton family at Thrushcross Grange until healed. This separation causes a rift in their friendship as Catherine begins to seek the friendship of the Linton children over Heathcliff's companionship. Catherine, motivated by the wealth and status of the Lintons, accepts a marriage proposal from Edgar. In parallel to these events, Hindley marries and has a son named Hareton. His wife Frances dies shortly after giving birth, sending Hindley spiralling down a path of gambling and alcohol abuse.

Catherine's love for Edgar is superficial, but while she loves Heathcliff deeply and passionately, he cannot provide her financial security and material wealth like Edgar can. When Heathcliff overhears Catherine telling Nelly about her engagement and how she cannot marry Heathcliff despite loving him, he runs away from Wuthering Heights.

née: French for 'born,' used to introduce someone's original surname before marriage.

Regales: to entertain or amuse someone by recounting a story.

~ SnapRevise® ~

A violent storm rages while Catherine chases after him, but she cannot find him. She catches a cold from the wet weather and passes her illness on to Edgar's parents who die soon after. She is tortured by her separation from Heathcliff, but with him gone and Edgar waiting, she marries the latter. She then moves to her husband's estate (Thrushcross Grange), bringing Nelly with her.

Three years after he left, Heathcliff returns in possession of the wealth and learning he once lacked. He lives with Hindley at Wuthering Heights (despite their previous grievances), paying him rent but carefully allowing the older man to gamble his assets away. He has returned to be near Catherine and spends a lot of time at Thrushcross Grange. Edgar's younger sister Isabella quickly becomes infatuated with him. Although Heathcliff does not love (or even like) Isabella, he entertains her affections as she is Edgar's heir. Infuriated by Heathcliff's proximity to his wife and sister, Edgar urges Catherine to make a choice between himself and Heathcliff, leading to a major argument between all parties.

Catherine falls ill and becomes delirious (we also learn she is seven-months pregnant!). While everyone is preoccupied with her decline, Heathcliff and Isabella elope, prompting Edgar to renounce all ties to his sister. Not long after, Nelly receives a letter from Isabella, detailing her new life at Wuthering Heights and how she regrets marrying Heathcliff (who is abusive).

Nelly decides to pay Wuthering Heights a visit. There, Heathcliff asks Nelly to let him see Catherine but Nelly is hesitant, worried for Catherine's health and marriage. However, eventually she agrees to convey a letter on his behalf and facilitate a visit while Edgar is out of the house. During this brief stay, we see Heathcliff's controlled brutality; he is careful not to grant Isabella grounds for divorce (which was very rare in the 1700s anyhow!) despite his hatred of her.

Heathcliff's final meeting with Catherine takes place at Thrushcross Grange while Edgar is at church; the two of them discuss their past and regrets. Upon his return, Edgar is furious but Catherine faints, so he tends to her before turning on Heathcliff. Heathcliff agrees to wait in the garden until the next morning for news about Catherine's health.

Catherine passes away that night after giving birth to her daughter, also named Catherine Linton (again we'll call her Cathy to avoid confusion). Sensing this loss, Heathcliff urges her spirit to haunt him so that he is not alone. In the wake of Catherine's death, Isabella takes advantage of the confusion to escape and moves south of London where she gives birth to Heathcliff's son, Linton Heathcliff. Six months after his sister's death, Hindley passes away too. Heathcliff claims ownership of Wuthering Heights as Hindley had mortgaged the property against Heathcliff to fund his gambling. Hareton, having inherited his father's debt, is also under Heathcliff's guardianship.

Twelve peaceful years pass until Isabella falls ill and dies, leaving her son Linton in the care of Edgar. Previously confined to Thrushcross Grange, Cathy takes advantage of her father's absence to wander the moors. She finds Wuthering Heights and meets Hareton. When she discovers he is her cousin, she is both shocked and upset. Shortly after, Hareton becomes Linton's servant when Heathcliff forces the sickly boy to move to Wuthering Heights.

Against her father's wishes, Cathy and Linton begin to send notes to one another, which evolve into love letters (while this sounds romantic, it is heavily suggested Heathcliff is editing Linton's writing!). Upon discovering the letters, Nelly burns them. Cathy is disheartened by their ceased correspondence but learns about the past and Heathcliff's malevolent character from her father. Nelly advises her to be sensible and look after her father's ailing health rather than focusing on romance.

On a walk one morning, Cathy and Nelly encounter Heathcliff who attributes Linton's poor health to Cathy's lack of affection, successfully guilting her into coming to Wuthering Heights the next day. Linton exaggerates his illness to play on Cathy's sympathies, so she continues to secretly visit him in the evenings.

She is discovered by Nelly who once more who tells Edgar. He bans her from visiting Wuthering Heights but allows Linton to visit Thrushcross Grange. However, he is too weak to travel between the estates, so Heathcliff 'encourages' Linton to write letters to Edgar about how much he misses Cathy. Edgar's illness worsens and Heathcliff continues to influence a marriage between his son and Cathy to secure Linton's position as heir to Thrushcross Grange. Finally, Cathy and Linton meet again under Nelly's supervision, but Linton's health is deteriorating quickly. Cathy is disappointed by this meeting but does not reveal this to her father.

On their next meeting, Heathcliff ambushes Cathy and Nelly, luring and trapping them at Wuthering Heights. Nelly is locked up for days and cannot intervene while Cathy and Linton are married. Nelly is eventually freed and Cathy escapes a few days later. They return to Thrushcross Grange where Cathy spends time with her father before he dies.

Heathcliff brings Cathy back to Wuthering Heights. He tells Nelly he dug up Catherine's grave to see her and can feel her presence everywhere. With Edgar dead and Linton dying, both Thrushcross Grange and Wuthering Heights will be Heathcliff's.

In the present day (less than a year after Edgar's death) Cathy has become cold and closed off. Linton has passed away and Cathy hates everything (and everyone) at Wuthering Heights. Lockwood visits Wuthering Heights before leaving for London, bringing Cathy a note from Nelly. The young lady cannot reply as Heathcliff destroyed all her books and writing materials. Hareton, who is teaching himself to read, tries to give her some books but she refuses them out of spite.

A year later, Lockwood is in the vicinity and decides to visit Thrushcross Grange and Wuthering Heights. He learns Nelly has been allowed to resume employment at Wuthering Heights and that Heathcliff passed away three months prior. Before his death, he renounced his quest for revenge and sunk into a delirious mania, regularly seeing Catherine's ghost. Furthermore, Cathy and Hareton have reconciled; she is teaching him to read and they are to be married soon. As he leaves Wuthering Heights for the final time, Lockwood visits the gravesite where Heathcliff, Catherine, and Edgar all lie buried together.

Section 2

Background Information

The life of Emily Brontë

Emily Brontë, born in 1818, was the fifth of six children born to Anglican minister Patrick Brontë and his wife Maria Branwell Brontë. Early life in Haworth (a small village in northern England) situated Brontë amongst the wilderness and moors that she later immortalised in her works. She may have also associated this setting with the passing of her mother early in her life. After this tragedy, the children were cared for by their extremely religious maternal aunt Elizabeth Branwell.

At the age of six, Brontë briefly attended school but was quickly removed after an outbreak of tuberculosis took the lives of her two oldest sisters. Brontë and her siblings, now consisting of Charlotte (the eldest), Branwell (the only son), and Anne (the youngest), were all educated at home. This may have been what sparked their propensity for writing. They enjoyed creating stories together, developing their craft in early works such as *Tales of Glass Town, Angria, and Gondal.*

Following in her sister Charlotte's footsteps, Brontë sought to become a teacher but soon realised her health could not cope with the demanding workload. In 1842, she and Charlotte studied in Brussels to improve their French and German, planning to open their own school. Her excellence in her studies secured her an offer of employment in Brussels, but the death of their aunt brought both sisters back home.

In 1844, they tried to open a school from their house, however it was difficult to gather students because of their remote location. After this setback, Brontë began to compile poems she had written over the years into two books. Upon Charlotte's insistence, all three sisters published their poetry using masculine pseudonyms, Emily's bring 'Ellis Bell.'

In 1847, she published her only novel, *Wuthering Heights (*alongside Anne's *Agnes Grey),* under the Bell pseudonym. It received a mixed response, some commending it for its brilliance and others appalled by its dark and disturbing nature. Less than a year later, before the novel could reach the pinnacle of its success, Brontë's only brother Branwell died very suddenly. After his funeral, Brontë developed tuberculosis and died in December of 1848 at only 30 years old.

Plagued by loss from the early deaths of many of her family members, Brontë reflects the uncertainty and grief of her life in *Wuthering Heights.* Her **perfusion** of Gothic and supernatural elements (such as ghosts) in the text can perhaps speak to her longing for her lost family members.

Perfusion: having something spread throughout, like blood through a body.

Why set *Wuthering Heights* in the 18th century?

Brontë wrote *Wuthering Heights* in the 1840s during the early Victorian era, a period characterised by rapid industrialisation and intensive change in both rural and urban lifestyles. However, *Wuthering Heights* takes place during the mid-18th century to the very early 19th century, reflecting a time when rural life would not have been disrupted by the social, economic, and lifestyle shifts of the **Industrial Revolution.**

Industrial Revolution: an era marked by intense technological advancement and transition to machine manufacturing.

There is a lot of speculation regarding why Brontë chose this specific period, but the general consensus is that it was a fitting context given the prevalence of Gothic literature in the 1700s. The 18th century was the most potent time for the development of Gothicism and Romanticism in their influence on literature. Famous Romantic and Gothic texts such as *The Rime of the Ancient Mariner* (1798) by Samuel Taylor Coleridge and *The Castle of Otranto* (1764) by Horace Walpole were published during this time, and staple Gothic horror novels such as Mary Shelly's *Frankenstein* (1818) were set in this period. By the late 18th century, Romanticism became widely acknowledged in art, philosophy, and literature, largely due to its opposition to the Industrial Revolution and its inspiration from the French Revolution.

What else happened in the 18th century?

King George III reigned for 60 years as the monarch of Great Britain and Ireland during the late 18th century. During this period, **imperialist** attitudes permeated British society and several significant wars such as the Seven Years' War and the American War of Independence were fought. However, very little of the political context of the Georgian era actually reveals itself in the text.

Imperialist: a policy expanding an empire's power and influence through colonising other people and countries.

More important was the social context of the time, especially in the treatment of people of colour which features strongly in the first half of the novel. Heathcliff was brought to Wuthering Heights in the early 1770s, which coincides with a significant ruling dissuading the transport of slaves from England. Lord Mansfield ruled in 1772 that no slave could be forcibly transported from England against their will. Although this did not end slavery, it was an important milestone that paved the way for the eventual Slavery Abolition Act in 1833. Heathcliff's origins are unknown with characters speculating that he may have been of Romani heritage or "a little **Lascar,** or an American or Spanish castaway." The outrage shown by the Earnshaw family upon his arrival soon mellows into a begrudging acceptance, reflecting the contextual attitudes of the English populace.

Lascar: a dated term for a sailor from the Indian subcontinent.

England during the 18th and 19th centuries was a classist society that believed in a prescribed hierarchy of roles. Brontë reflects this in her social division of the Lintons, Earnshaws, and their servants.

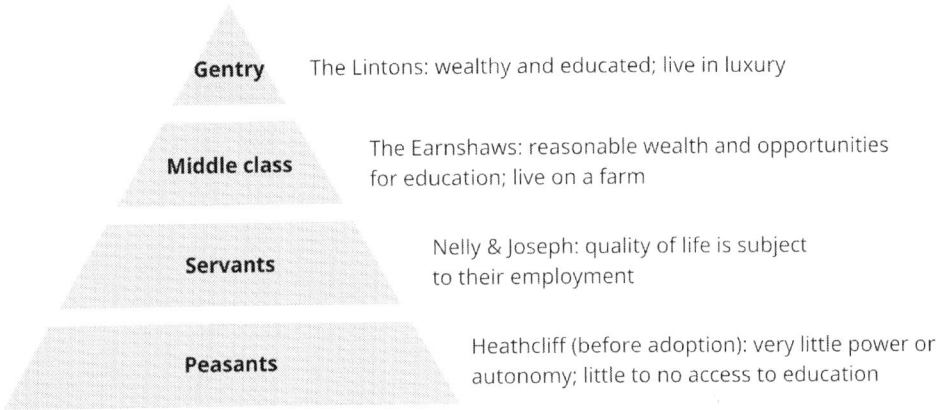

Gentry — The Lintons: wealthy and educated; live in luxury

Middle class — The Earnshaws: reasonable wealth and opportunities for education; live on a farm

Servants — Nelly & Joseph: quality of life is subject to their employment

Peasants — Heathcliff (before adoption): very little power or autonomy; little to no access to education

Social mobility was rare and often frowned upon. This was because the movement of an individual from a higher class usually involved an unfavourable marriage or vices such as gambling or drinking. Moving up from a lower class was incredibly difficult as people rarely earned enough to do this. In *Wuthering Heights,* Heathcliff changed classes multiple times, first from a peasant, to middle class under Old Mr Earnshaw's guardianship, then to being a servant under Hindley, and finally to a gentleman when he returned from his three-year disappearance. He is greatly disliked by others for various reasons, including his racial background – people of colour often did not have such wealth in this time – and his terrible attitude.

Social mobility: change in social class often through marriage or newfound wealth.

Inheritance and succession in the 18th century

Inheritance, wills, and estates are an aspect of 18th century life that becomes important later in the text. For peasants and servants, this was not often an issue as they did not own much. However, for wealthy and middle-class people, such as the Lintons and Earnshaws respectively, it was important to outline the line of succession of one's properties. Being the 18th century, male children were the preferred heirs, but (contrary to popular belief) women could also inherit estates.

When a man died, his assets would be given to his oldest male child, and from there that child could pass it on to his own heir and so on. However, Old Mr Linton designed a will that operated slightly differently.

Upon his death, Old Mr Linton's assets would be bequeathed to his only son, Edgar. However, there was a stipulation that instructed his property and wealth to be given to Isabella if Edgar had no male children. This is why Thrushcross Grange did not immediately pass on to Cathy (Edgar's daughter). Since Isabella died before Edgar, she does not inherit (shown by the dotted outline) and his assets would then become Linton's because he was Isabella's son and Old Mr Linton's only male grandchild. It is highly likely that if Isabella had a daughter, then Cathy would have inherited her father's estate.

Similarly, in the Earnshaw family, wealth is inherited by the eldest sons. However, Hindley gambles his wealth away so Hareton (his son) has nothing to inherit (shown by the dotted outline). Since Hindley mortaged his assets against Heathcliff, Heathcliff can claim ownership of Wuthering Heights (Hindley's estate).

Thurshcross Grange

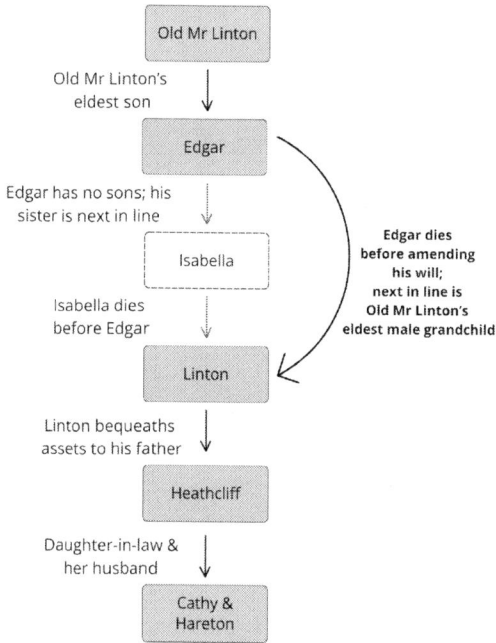

Old Mr Linton

Old Mr Linton's eldest son →

Edgar

Edgar has no sons; his sister is next in line →

Isabella

Isabella dies before Edgar →

Linton

Linton bequeaths assets to his father →

Heathcliff

Daughter-in-law & her husband →

Cathy & Hareton

Edgar dies before amending his will; next in line is Old Mr Linton's eldest male grandchild

Wuthering Heights

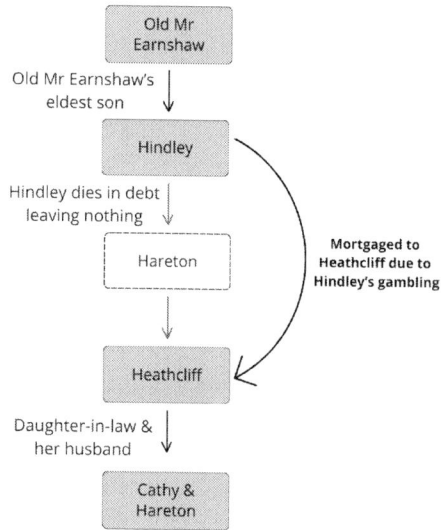

Old Mr Earnshaw

Old Mr Earnshaw's eldest son →

Hindley

Hindley dies in debt leaving nothing →

Hareton

Heathcliff

Daughter-in-law & her husband →

Cathy & Hareton

Mortgaged to Heathcliff due to Hindley's gambling

This is a very confusing concept, but you can refer back to this diagram when the issue of succession comes up in the text.

The Gothic genre

The Gothic is often referred to as the 'dark side of Romanticism,' as it is a genre of art and literature that focuses on the disturbing and oftentimes **macabre** aspects of humanity. It is characterised by dark and lonesome settings, powerful natural forces, (potentially) supernatural influences, and many mysteries. Both Romantic and Gothic literature glorify natural landscapes in comparison to urbanisation, but where Romanticism features aesthetically pleasing imagery, Gothicism prefers daunting, **sublime** environments.

Another key feature of Gothicism is its peculiar and dark characters. Gothic writers tend to forgo the beauty and predominantly positive nature of Romantic characters, opting to embrace their characters' flaws and negative traits. Many Gothic heroes fall under the **archetype** of the **Byronic hero** (named for the works of Lord Byron). The Byronic hero is often moody, cynical with a hatred for their society, and has incredible intelligence. A Byronic hero is rarely a true hero due to their many red flags but is often capable of attracting the heroine due to his mysterious charms and amazingly good looks.

Heathcliff is the **epitome** of a Byronic hero. He is cruel, holds extreme hatred for almost everyone around him (to the point of physical and mental abuse), and has an air of mystery, as nobody knows where he came from or where he went in his three years away. He is also a strong and handsome young man whose charms attract the love of Catherine and subsequently the affection of Isabella.

To complement this hero, Gothic literature also features heroines who shirk the constraints of acceptable society and tend to be well-attuned to their sublime surroundings. Like most Gothic characters, they are highly emotional and a little bit 'wild' as they chase after some larger unknown. Catherine embodies this characterisation as she always longs to be outside on the moors and takes solace from her unsatisfying lifestyle through her connection to Heathcliff. She always craves something more no matter where she is – for example her desire for social standing and wealth while at Wuthering Heights, and to enmesh her soul with both Heathcliff and the moors as she approaches death. This deep connection to the natural world is also found in many Romantic characters; however, Catherine's self-destruction and lack of satisfaction contributes to her characterisation as a Gothic heroine.

Macabre: ghastly or gruesome, often related to the subject of death.

Sublime: awe-inspiring beauty; unparalleled.

Archetype: a pattern of typical characteristics (e.g. a villain archetype).

Byronic hero: a troubled variant of the Romantic hero who will often act for the sake of their own interests such as in pursuit of revenge.

Epitome: a perfect example.

Section 3

Chapter-by-Chapter Analysis

Chapter I

The year is 1801 and Mr Lockwood, a tenant at Thrushcross Grange, goes to visit his landlord, Heathcliff, at Wuthering Heights. Lockwood explains to the reader that the name "Wuthering" describes the powerful, untameable winds and "stormy weather" common at the estate's elevated point on the moors. He declares the setting as "beautiful [...] a perfect **misanthropist's** Heaven" indicating its isolation.

Misanthropist: someone who dislikes human interaction and prefers solitude.

The chapter begins with an introduction between the two men. Lockwood seems curious about Heathcliff and his reserved nature, but upon meeting sees Heathcliff's **brusque** demeanour. Lockwood takes interest in Heathcliff's family history as he notes the house was built in 1500. However, Heathcliff commands him to "walk in" (albeit in an uninviting manner) and sends Joseph, the elderly groundskeeper, to tend to Lockwood's horse.

Brusque: abrupt to the point of rudeness; rough.

As he surveys his surroundings, Lockwood realises the house's layout is unusual with the kitchen hidden away. He can hear other people inside but cannot see them. Instead, he focuses on the architecture and décor, noticing that it would not be unusual for a "homely, northern farmer." He also becomes aware of the many dogs Heathcliff keeps in the house.

Once again turning his attention to Heathcliff, Lockwood describes him with the racial label of "gipsy," which at that time was used to describe people of darker skin tones and Romani heritage. The importance of this label lies in how Lockwood contrasts Heathcliff's appearance with his "gentleman[ly]" manners and clothes" and "handsome figure." He also speculates about Heathcliff's "rather **morose**" and reserved character, trying to draw similarities between two of them.

Morose: sullen; gloomy sadness.

We can see that Lockwood desires to form connections with those around him, yet this proves difficult for him. He recounts his prior experience with love, where his shy behaviour cost him a relationship and contributed to his reputation as a heartless man. By likening himself to Heathcliff and vice versa, it is clear that he wants to understand more about his landlord and seeks a level of solace in knowing there are others in the world who may be misunderstood like him.

Heathcliff is next portrayed in an animalistic fashion when he growls "in unison" with his dog. This is a part of the many subtle techniques Brontë uses to construct Heathcliff's wild and tumultuous character in accordance with the Byronic hero archetype.

Left alone for a moment while Heathcliff disappears in search of Joseph, Lockwood makes faces at some of the dogs causing them to attack him. The attack is soon subdued and Lockwood escapes unharmed. Heathcliff is angry at first, but quickly relaxes and offers his tenant wine, claiming that he and his dogs are inexperienced with entertaining guests. As they converse, Lockwood notes that Heathcliff is quite intelligent and plans a subsequent visit for the next day, despite knowing Heathcliff "evidently wished no repetition of his intrusion."

Analysis

In her description of the setting **Brontë uses pathetic fallacy, a staple technique of Gothic literature, to showcase the sublime natural forces that surround Wuthering Heights.** For example: the "atmospheric **tumult**" and "the power of the north wind, blowing" over the moors, while the plants have "gaunt thorns all stretching their limbs one way." This personification conveys the unbridled forces of nature that dominate the novel and presents the setting as a living and important element of the text. The building itself, with "narrow windows" and "jutting stones," creates jagged and foreboding imagery for the reader, which further ties into the pervasive Gothic ambience of *Wuthering Heights*.

Pathetic fallacy: to describe inanimate objects with human feelings and conduct.

Tumult: a loud and often confused uproar emitted by a crowd of people.

Chapter II

Lockwood is inclined to forgo his second visit to rest by the fire but is displaced by a servant cleaning the fireplace. He treks to Wuthering Heights and arrives just as snow starts falling. Angered by the shut door and lack of shelter, Lockwood resolves to enter the estate but is interrupted by Joseph. The groundskeeper informs him that Heathcliff is away and the "missis" inside will not open the door. As he tries the door again, Lockwood meets a young man who leads him through the back of the house and into the front room again.

The missis (a young woman) is present but does not offer him the level of hospitality he is expecting, continuing to ignore him even when he tries to make conversation. The man tells him to sit, and Lockwood once again attempts conversation with the woman he mistakenly perceives to be Heathcliff's wife. Her replies are given "more repellingly than Heathcliff himself," in a short and sharp manner. When she turns into the light, Lockwood is surprised to see she is beautiful but appears miserable. Diverting his attention to the young man, he tries to deduce whether he is a servant or not, noticing that his "shabby" appearance confirms this, but his "haughty" behaviour does not.

Heathcliff's arrival brings some relief to Lockwood and he asks for a servant to help guide him home through the snowstorm. Heathcliff refuses and "savagely" orders tea made. His tone is so rude that Lockwood's entire perception of Heathcliff pivots. He no longer sees him as a "capital fellow" and is suddenly repulsed.

The "universal scowl" on everyone's face at the dinner table perplexes him further; he cannot believe that this unhappiness is their daily norm. To dispel the awkwardness, he tries to compliment Heathcliff for building such a fulfilling life with his family and "amiable lady" (wife) so far away from society. Since his wife is dead, Heathcliff is shocked. Realising his mistake, Lockwood backtracks and guesses that the young lady may instead be married to Heathcliff's son, presumably, the young man.

Heathcliff explains with an air of condescension that the woman is indeed his daughter-in-law (which makes her Mrs Heathcliff), but his son is dead, and that the man seated with them "assuredly" isn't his son. The young man, visibly humiliated, introduces himself as Hareton Earnshaw and demands respect. Ignoring this, Heathcliff instructs him to tend to the sheep as the blizzard rolls in.

Lockwood resumes his requests for a guide to walk him back to Thrushcross Grange; however, he is sidelined as Joseph and Mrs Heathcliff begin arguing. Finally, Lockwood decides to set out alone, taking a lantern with him under the promise that he will return it in the morning. Hareton decides to help him for at least part of the way, and Mrs Heathcliff agrees that this is reasonable. Heathcliff is angered by this as he does not want to risk losing one of the few people who help maintain the grounds.

Joseph, under the impression that Lockwood is stealing the lantern, encourages some of the dogs to chase after him, and they manage to pin him down. After fending off the dogs, Lockwood is thus forced to spend the night at Wuthering Heights under the care of the housekeeper, Zillah.

Analysis

This chapter gives the reader better insight into different characters and their values. For example, Joseph uses religious language in his everyday speech. From the few lines of dialogue from him so far, we see that he is a devout Christian and has an overpowering fear of spiritual condemnation. During his argument with Mrs Heathcliff, he provokes her by saying she'll "goa raight to t' divil" (go right to the devil) like her mother. After implying her deceased mother is in hell, Mrs Heathcliff threatens him with "Black Art" (witchcraft). Joseph exhibits "sincere horror," responding "oh, wicked, wicked! [...] may the Lord deliver us from evil!" **Such deep-rooted, pious fears are a significant aspect of Joseph's characterisation and Brontë contrasts his religious devotion to the 'devil-may-care' attitudes of other characters such as Heathcliff.**

Reprehensible: recognised as bad and deserving of criticism.

On the topic of Heathcliff, his character has been established through Lockwood's eyes as morally **reprehensible** and utterly detestable. He values himself and believes others should be there to serve his purposes, hence why he was keen to keep Hareton off the moors. He mistreats his daughter-in-law and gives her "a look of hatred" upon introduction to Lockwood.

Such disregard for social norms and propriety thoroughly irks Lockwood. When his polite conversation is met by "an **austere** silence" and scowling, Lockwood believes Hareton and Mrs Heathcliff are sullen and brusque like Heathcliff. This notion is only challenged when Hareton volunteers to go out with him, and Mrs Heathcliff backs up this decision.

Austere: somber; cold in manner.

Chapter III

Zillah leads Lockwood up to a bedroom, advising him to be silent as Heathcliff does not like visitors in this room. He comes across a stack of old books on a ledge with three names scratched over and over into the paint: *Catherine Earnshaw, Catherine Heathcliff,* and *Catherine Linton.* As he falls asleep, his candle begins to burn one of the books, so he wakes and puts out the fire. He picks up a book and realises it belongs to Catherine Earnshaw, written about 25 years ago.

He picks up another book, Catherine's diary, and reads an account of "an awful Sunday" after the death of Catherine's father, where her brother Hindley was revelling in the power he now held as the master of the house. He would force the children to listen to Joseph's sermons and punish them for the slightest offences, such as making a sound. He refused to allow Heathcliff to dine with them, swearing to "reduce him to his right place" (the status of a servant), unlike how he was treated under the care of Catherine's father.

Lockwood once again falls asleep, and this time has a nightmare about being attacked by Joseph and the congregation during a boring sermon. He wakes up to the sound of a branch tapping against the window but cannot open the window to move it. In frustration he smashes the pane and reaches out for the branch but is instead surprised to feel "the fingers of a little, ice-cold hand." A voice asks him to let her in, claiming to be Catherine Linton, refusing to let go of his hand until he does. Under the pretence that he will let her in, he convinces her to let go before he blocks the hole in the window with a pile of books. The ghost pushes the books away and mourns that she has been a "**waif** for twenty years" as Lockwood screams, drawing Heathcliff to the room.

Waif: uncared for with no place to belong to; often refers to children.

Standing in the darkness, Lockwood confesses his presence to Heathcliff and tells him he saw the ghost of Catherine. Upon realising that Catherine and Heathcliff used to be close, he tries to change the subject, but it is already too late as Heathcliff is overcome with "violent emotion." He ushers Lockwood out and tells him he will follow soon. Unsure of where to go, Lockwood waits outside the room and witnesses Heathcliff beckon Catherine's ghost, his "heart's darling," through the window, but the only thing coming through was snow.

In the morning, everything appears normal once again, including Heathcliff's continued, terrible treatment of Mrs Heathcliff who he admonishes for being "worthless." He walks Lockwood back down to the edge of Thrushcross Grange, allowing him to complete the journey alone. At home, everyone rejoices to see Lockwood as they thought he died in the blizzard.

Analysis

The ghost of Catherine is our first encounter with the supernatural. **Gothic literature often engages with supernatural elements and _Wuthering Heights_ uses this to explore the line between life and death,** and the connection between people and nature. Although Catherine has been dead for many years, a stranger such as Lockwood is still able to sense her through her books and the setting, revealing the depth of the connection she had to them.

An interesting way to interpret this scene is to consider the house as the land of the living, and the stormy moors outside to be a realm beyond life. I choose these words carefully as death connotes being unable to interact with the living world. However, if we view these different settings as separate planes of existence, we can see that Catherine is desperately trying to return to what she once had and, through his yearning for her, Heathcliff wants the same. By puncturing a hole through the window, Lockwood briefly broke the 'barrier' that separated the two worlds, but this spell ended almost as quickly as it began.

Another interpretation of this scene asserts the ability of emotional connection to transcend life and death. (This interpretation could function as a possible thesis for your essays!) The desperation of Catherine's ghost when she begs Lockwood to let her in is amplified by her repetition of this singular request. Whether the reason she wishes to be let in is to reunite with Heathcliff or to be inside her childhood home, a common thread is the strength of her bond with both, persisting even after her death. Furthermore, Heathcliff's pining shows that despite Catherine's death, almost two decades ago, he still loves her and feels connected to her.

Chapter IV

Determined to remain in solitude, Lockwood avoids social interaction for some time, but before long his curiosity compels him to seek the company of Ellen 'Nelly' Dean, the housekeeper at Thrushcross Grange. He asks her to tell him about the residents of Wuthering Heights, considering that she lived there for many years and even nursed Mrs Catherine Heathcliff née Linton (this is Mr Heathcliff's daughter-in-law who I will now refer to as Cathy). Nelly explains that the Linton family used to live at Thrushcross Grange, and the Earnshaws at Wuthering Heights. Cathy is the daughter of the late Mr Edgar Linton and Mrs Catherine Linton née Earnshaw (this Catherine is the ghost from last chapter, and I'll refer to her as Catherine). This can be confusing, so feel free to return to the family tree on page 1 for guidance!

From here, the text consists of Lockwood's recount of Nelly's story, and is therefore in Nelly's perspective.

Nelly's story begins in her childhood at Wuthering Heights. Her mother nursed Hindley and as a result she grew up with the Earnshaw children, helping with odd jobs around the house. One day, Old Mr Earnshaw decides he "shall walk there and back: sixty miles each way" to Liverpool, promising to bring home a fiddle for Hindley (age 14), a horse-riding whip for Catherine (age 6), and fruits for Nelly. Late on the third night after his departure, he returns carrying with him a "dirty, ragged, black-haired child." Old Mr Earnshaw had picked up the homeless child on the streets of Liverpool and, determined not to leave him to suffer there, had decided to bring him home. Nelly is instructed to "wash it, and clean it, and let it sleep with the children."

At this point, everyone in the household except Old Mr Earnshaw hates the boy, and this sentiment multiplies when the children find out that Hindley's fiddle was broken, and Catherine's whip had been lost while her father was helping the boy. Since they refuse to sleep with him nearby, Nelly leaves the boy on the landing of the staircase, and he makes his way to Old Mr Earnshaw in the darkness. Confessing to leaving him there, Nelly is banished from the house for a few days and upon her return finds that things have changed a lot.

The boy has been named 'Heathcliff' (which acts as both his first and last name), after one of the Earnshaw children who had died, and he has now befriended Catherine. However, Hindley and Old Mrs Earnshaw still dislike him, the former making efforts to inconvenience him, and the latter allowing her son's behaviour. Nelly describes Heathcliff as a "sullen, patient child; hardened [...] to ill-treatment," and who quickly became Old Mr Earnshaw's favourite child. Whenever Hindley hurt the boy, his father would always take Heathcliff's side, breeding further dislike between them.

Within two years of Heathcliff's arrival, Old Mrs Earnshaw passes away. Hindley begins to view "his father as an oppressor rather than a friend, and Heathcliff as a **usurper** of his parent's affections and his privileges." Nelly's dislike towards the boy changes after she cares for him through a bout of measles, since she notices that he rarely complains despite being the sickest of the three children and "thus Hindley lost his last ally."

Usurper: a person who takes another's place, usually with force or by ill-gotten means.

She goes on to recount the way Heathcliff would blackmail Hindley to get what he wanted. At this time, she thinks him "not **vindictive**" since he rarely complained, but later realises she was wrong.

Vindictive: showing a desire to harm or take revenge.

Analysis

The use of the word 'it' to describe Heathcliff when he was first brought to the house is **ostracising**. It shows that the family, aside from Old Mr Earnshaw, saw him as an object rather than a person. He is called a "stupid little thing" and bullied by Catherine and Hindley.

Ostracise: to exclude from a group.

A significant reason for this maltreatment is due to racism which presents as fear and disgust in most of the family. This can be seen through Old Mrs Earnshaw's use of the racial slur "gipsy brat" and Old Mr Earnshaw's description of the boy being "as dark almost as if it came from the devil." The immediate difference of Heathcliff's physical appearance was jarring to the family, especially because **in this context, racist beliefs perpetuated the notion that people of colour were inferior.** This was only exacerbated by Heathcliff's ascension to the position of Old Mr Earnshaw's favourite child.

Although he and Catherine soon became close, there are various reasons behind why Hindley continued to hate him. Previously the only and eldest son, Hindley would have been quite accustomed to having his way and being his father's sole heir. However, the introduction of Heathcliff challenged his standing within the family. Although Heathcliff was not a biological child of the Earnshaws, he was treated the same way, thus displacing some of the affection Hindley believed was reserved for himself. With his mother's passing, the gap between him and his father only grew wider as Heathcliff

Acrimony:
bitterness and resentment.

maintained his role as the favourite child. This childish **acrimony** foreshadows the conflict between Hindley and Heathcliff that will escalate later in the novel.

Chapter V

As Old Mr Earnshaw's health declines, he is prone to fits of anger and violence against anyone (especially Hindley) who slights Heathcliff. Hindley is sent off to college and Nelly reveals Catherine's "mischief" and how she enjoyed provoking her father in his final days. She also recounts the close relationship between Heathcliff and Catherine; the "greatest punishment [...] was to keep her separate from him" and that Heathcliff "would do *her* bidding in anything."

One night, the family and servants sat by the fire, Catherine leaning on her father's knee, and Heathcliff resting his head on her lap. She sings her father to sleep, and sometime later Joseph decides to wake him for prayers. Upon discovering Old Mr Earnshaw has passed away, Catherine and Heathcliff retreat to their bedroom while Nelly calls the doctor. When she returns, she saw the children consoling each other, further cementing their deep bond.

Analysis

Solace:
consolation to alleviate distress or discomfort.

This chapter provides insight into the closeness of Heathcliff and Catherine's relationship. Being the only two children on the property, they are inclined to play with each other and form a great friendship. However, the closeness of this connection is further evident when they seek **solace** in each other rather than in the adults around them. This reveals how well they understand each other and sets up their close bond and love as adults later in the text.

Chapter VI

Hindley returns to Wuthering Heights for his father's funeral. To everyone's surprise he is now married, and the master of the estate. His wife, Frances, appears to be frivolous and "half silly" in Nelly's eyes. Frances expresses a dislike towards Heathcliff, rekindling her new husband's **animosity** towards the boy. As such, Heathcliff is no longer permitted an education and is now put to work on the farm, diminishing him to the status of servant.

Animosity: hostility; a strong hatred.

Catherine initially taught Heathcliff whatever she was learning and together the two of them would escape to the moors, warranting punishment that they would forget the "minute they were together again." One night, the children are nowhere to be found, and Hindley orders for the doors bolted shut, leaving them outside for the night. Nelly keeps her window open, ready to bring them inside when they arrive, but is shocked to see Heathcliff return alone.

He explains that he and Catherine ran to Thrushcross Grange to spy on the Linton children, and while they were there they began taunting the Lintons. Unsure what was making the noise, the Lintons set their dog out and Catherine was bitten on the ankle. The children were brought inside Thrushcross Grange where the Lintons lay an onslaught of insults upon Heathcliff, calling him "quite unfit for a decent house!" for his appearance and ill-manners. He begins to curse at them again and is thrown out of the house, told to return to Wuthering Heights while they care for Catherine.

The next morning, Old Mr Linton visits Wuthering Heights to inform Hindley about the events. Heathcliff's punishment is that he is never to speak to Catherine again, or else he will be dismissed.

Analysis

Hindley's return to Wuthering Heights is **marred** by his tyrannical and controlling behaviour. To escape this, Heathcliff and Catherine spend a lot of time engaging in mischief outside. At this time, in the late 18th century, such behaviour would be considered unsavoury for a young lady like Catherine. It is also shameful for her to be spending time with a servant, especially one of Heathcliff's background. This is evident by the Lintons' reaction to finding them together. They are initially in denial, and shame Hindley's "carelessness" at letting his sister "grow up in absolute heathenism" with Heathcliff. Isabella Linton compares Heathcliff to "the son of the fortune-teller that stole" from her, and Heathcliff is called a "gipsy" and "a wicked boy," this time by Mrs Linton. All these **repudiations** contribute to Heathcliff's contempt towards the Lintons in the future.

Marred: negatively impacted by; ruined.

Repudiation: rejection or renoucement.

Another interesting observation to note is the difference in upbringing and personalities between the Linton children and Catherine and Heathcliff. The Lintons are refined but "cowardly" in comparison to Catherine and Heathcliff's wild behaviour.

This initial contrast between their lifestyles alludes to the greater conflict of nature versus civilisation explored in the text. The Linton children are brought up as 'proper' members of society, spending their evenings indoors, attending church regularly, and attaining an education – a clear representation of what was seen as the ideal for their social standing at the time. Meanwhile, Heathcliff and Catherine run wild on the moors, unhindered by the wind, harsh weather, or even the punishments they face at home – they are far more attuned to the sublime of nature than civilisation. I'll expand on this in the Key Themes section of this guide (see page 73).

Chapter VII

Catherine returns to Wuthering Heights five weeks later, her ankle healed, and her entire person reworked into a 'proper lady.' For the first time in years, Hindley seems happy to see his sister as her manners have greatly improved. He calls Heathcliff out to see Catherine and she is shocked to see him even more unkempt than before, commenting that she is now used to the Lintons' manners and cleanliness. She hugs and kisses him, but he does not respond to her affection, instead angered by Catherine's comments on his dirtiness. Exclaiming "I shall be as dirty as I please," he runs away, leaving Catherine confused, and Hindley and Frances relieved. Plans have been made for the Linton children to visit the next morning under the condition that the "naughty swearing boy" Heathcliff is kept away from them.

That night, Nelly sits by the fire and reminisces on Old Mr Earnshaw's "fondness for Heathcliff," who is now treated like scum. She finds him in the stable and offers to help him neaten his appearance to spend time with Catherine, but he does not respond. The next morning, once the family has departed for church, he comes to Nelly and requests that she make him presentable. He voices his desire to be more like Edgar Linton, in manners, wealth, and appearance, wishing he "had light hair and a fair skin." Nelly comforts him by highlighting his height and strength, and before long Heathcliff turns his frown upside down.

Prepared to apologise to Catherine while she is in a good mood, Heathcliff walks into the room where is spending time with the Linton children. Coincidentally, Hindley opens the other door and sees him, ordering Joseph to keep him out of the way until the children are gone. Edgar comments that Heathcliff's hair is long, like a "colt's mane," and in a fit of rage, Heathcliff throws hot applesauce at the boy. Hindley takes him away and punishes him, while Catherine scolds Edgar for speaking to Heathcliff. Soon they forget about the entire ordeal and settle for the meal.

Later that night, a Christmas band comes to visit, and while everyone is busy celebrating Catherine sneaks upstairs to be with Heathcliff. Nelly eventually coaxes them down and agrees to hide Heathcliff in the kitchen to allow him a meal. Sitting sullenly in the kitchen, the boy vows that he will get revenge on Hindley, no matter how long he must wait.

In the present day, Nelly prepares to turn in for the night as it's already 11pm, but Lockwood urges her to continue her story.

Analysis

This chapter is the clear start of Heathcliff's plans to exact revenge on Hindley. It provides context for his immense dislike towards the Linton children – Edgar in particular. He sees Edgar as weak and yet still superior to him, with infuriates him.

We also see a growing rift between Catherine and Heathcliff. The young lady is torn between her childhood friend and the new society she has been introduced to. We can see that Catherine greatly values her new material luxuries and is not keen to give them up. She avoids the dogs when she arrives back at Wuthering Heights, afraid they will soil her beautiful dress, and when she sees Heathcliff again she worries his dirtiness will transfer to her clothes. Heathcliff's conviction to remain dirty serves as a reminder of her previous lifestyle which she has supposedly forsaken. **Brontë's juxtaposition of cleanliness and dirtiness conveys a division between the two children and their social status.**

When Heathcliff is taken away for attacking Edgar, she admonishes Edgar at once, and spends her day in "purgatory" unable to see Heathcliff and begs that "he might be liberated." She puts on a different face in front of the Linton children compared to the authenticity she reveals to Heathcliff in the attic. This need to hide their friendship from everyone will soon cause a strain on both parties.

Chapter VIII

In June of a following year, Hareton Earnshaw is born, bringing immense joy to the household. However, the doctor advises the family that Frances will not make it through the next winter as she has been sick for many months. Hindley was adamant right until the moment of her death that she would recover, and in the following days devolved into a tyrant once again. Hareton was put under Nelly's care and all servants, except for herself and Joseph, abandoned the house because of Hindley's drinking and temper.

As time passed, Heathcliff took great delight in angering Hindley, watching as he "degrad[ed] himself past redemption" with rage. Catherine remained "headstrong," and eventually everyone except for Edgar Linton (who came to see Catherine) stopped visiting Wuthering Heights. Nelly notes Catherine's "wondrous constancy to old attachments" as Edgar struggled "to make an equally deep impression" on her compared to her affection for Heathcliff. At this point in the story, Catherine is 15, Heathcliff 16, and Edgar 18.

Nelly pauses the story to point out a portrait of the late Edgar Linton to Lockwood. She notes that a portrait of his wife (Catherine) used to hang beside it, but it is no longer there. Lockwood can see the resemblance the portrait holds to the young Mrs Heathcliff (Cathy) he met at Wuthering Heights.

Defame:

slander or

disparage; to

bad-mouth

someone.

Poignant:

deeply affecting

and laced with

sadness.

Continuing with her story, Nelly reveals that Catherine began to "adopt a double character." Adored by the Linton family, she would allow Edgar to **defame** Heathcliff for his rudeness, while at home Catherine acted similarly, with "small inclination to practise politeness [...] and restrain [her own] unruly nature." Meanwhile, Heathcliff lets himself deteriorate both physically and mentally, abandoning any desire to learn "with **poignant** though silent regret" and taking "grim" pleasure in avoiding people. He stops verbally acknowledging that he cares for Catherine and is also annoyed by her attempts at showing physical affection.

One day, while Hindley is away, Heathcliff decides to skip work in the fields to spend time with Catherine. However, Catherine has invited Edgar to visit. Disappointed, Heathcliff does not like to complain, but he shows her a calendar on which he marked the days she spent time with him and the days she spent with the Lintons. Irritated by his needy behaviour, she says he is boring because he is uneducated.

Their argument is cut short by Edgar's arrival, which is smooth and elegant in comparison to Heathcliff's subsequent departure. Nelly, remaining in the room to supervise, begins cleaning. Catherine asks her to leave, but Nelly refuses and Catherine pinches her. At first Catherine refuses to admit she hurt Nelly, but soon escalates to slap her as well. She shakes the infant Hareton and hits Edgar when he tries to calm her. Edgar is shocked by the "double fault of falsehood and violence which his idol had committed" (Catherine's lies and behaviour) and attempts to leave, but Catherine threatens to "cry [herself] sick!"

Eventually, although still shocked and afraid of her outburst, he decides to stay, and they talk quietly. By the time Hindley returns, drunk, Edgar and Catherine have confessed their love for each other.

Analysis

The rift between Catherine and Heathcliff widens as she grows closer to Edgar. Her complete disregard for his desire to spend time with her is a sign that she no longer understands him as well as she used to. This is a cause for conflict in their relationship as both parties want different things in life. Catherine wants material satisfaction and Heathcliff wants to be treated with respect like everyone else around him.

An important part of this chapter is Catherine's tumultuous display of violence. **Strong, uncontrollable emotions are a key part of Gothic literature** as it allows the reader to see the dark side of humanity. Catherine's ability to physically hurt people who care for her is concerning for two main reasons, the first being that it shows a lack of compassion and exhibits complete selfishness; we see her flawed character.

Secondly, in 18th century British context, such unrefined and discourteous behaviour, including hitting the man courting her, would be enough to disgrace her forever if she was a part of normal society. However, living out on the moors, so far away from proper society, her behaviour mirrors her troubled upbringing and is hence excused by Edgar in his love for her. His captivation is made clear by his vain attempts to leave – like a cat unable "to leave a mouse half killed, or a bird half eaten."

Catherine's violence can also be seen as a reflection of the dark atmosphere around her, as Wuthering Heights is constantly barraged with storms and powerful winds that can tear down anything in their path. Conversely, Edgar's subdued reaction is an indication of the stable yet emotionally restrained life he is used to.

Chapter IX

Hindley's drunken state leaves him a "madman," prone to various outbursts of both affection and rage, oftentimes directed towards his son Hareton. This time, in his careless anger, he drops the child over the banister at the top of the stairs. Heathcliff catches the boy, but Nelly notes from his expression that he instantly regrets it. He would have preferred to let Hareton die to have his revenge on Hindley.

Hindley resumes his drinking and Nelly takes Hareton to the kitchen. Heathcliff supposedly passes through, but later Nelly realises he is still in the room, silent and obscured. Catherine comes in and confesses to Nelly that Edgar Linton has proposed to her and that she has agreed to marry him. Nelly quizzes her on why she loves Edgar and comes to understand that Catherine is marrying him because he is rich and handsome and can make her "the greatest woman of the neighbourhood."

Despite this supposed good news, Catherine is still sad. She recounts a dream where she went to heaven and felt she did not belong there, comparing her current situation to the same feeling of displacement and unease. She blames Hindley for lowering Heathcliff's status so much that it would "degrade" her to marry him, no matter how much she loves him. She declares her love in perhaps the most famous quote from the text: "whatever our souls are made of, his and mine are the same." Here, Catherine also alludes to **Milo of Croton,** saying anyone who should separate her and Heathcliff would "meet the fate of Milo!" (This indirectly hints at her similarly tragic fate as she marries Edgar, effecting a rift in her relationship with Heathcliff who is regularly described with wolf-related imagery and influencing her downfall.)

Milo of Croton: a renowned ancient Greek wrestler; he tried to pull apart a tree with his bare hands, but got trapped and was killed by wolves.

At this point, Heathcliff silently gets up and leaves the room, having overheard the entire conversation. Nelly tells Catherine to be quiet, but the girl is unaware that Heathcliff has heard everything. Catherine explains that she plans to use Edgar's money to help Heathcliff escape Hindley's power over him.

When Joseph comes inside, searching for Heathcliff, Nelly realises he has disappeared and tells Catherine the truth. In a frenzy, she runs outside to find him, abandoning her dinner. Joseph joins the search as well, but the gate to the property is open and Heathcliff is nowhere to be found. Catherine goes back outside to wait for Heathcliff, refusing to come inside despite the vicious storm that rages through the moors. A tree is split in half by lightning and damages part of the roof, making Joseph pray for salvation.

Eventually, Catherine comes inside, drenched, and spends the night shivering by the fire. In the morning, Hindley finds out from Joseph about Edgar's visit and implores Catherine to tell him the whole truth about what happened the previous night. She begins to cry; she does not want to part with Heathcliff, but fears "perhaps, he's gone." A doctor is called as Catherine develops a fever and is "dangerously ill," and Nelly takes to nursing her back to health. Old Mrs Linton pays multiple visits and takes Catherine back to Thrushcross Grange to care for her. However, Catherine's illness passes onto both Mr and Mrs Linton, taking their lives shortly after.

In the three years following Heathcliff's departure, Catherine becomes increasingly selfish and demanding, and Hindley enables her behaviour in hopes of having her marry Edgar Linton sooner. Once they are married, Nelly is forced to move to Thrushcross Grange with Catherine, leaving five-year-old Hareton in the care of his father.

Presently, as it is late at night, Nelly pauses her story leaving Lockwood to ruminate on what he has learnt.

Analysis

This chapter is a crucial turning point of the novel as it describes the point when Catherine chooses Edgar over Heathcliff. Although she claims that nothing can separate her from him, she also insults Heathcliff, revealing that she values material wealth and status above her relationship with him. Brontë uses many different techniques to describe the deep connection between Heathcliff and Catherine; let's look at two powerful quotes from Catherine's monologue.

> QUOTES :
> "If all else perished, and he remained, I should still continue to be; and if all else remained, and he were annihilated, the universe would turn to a mighty stranger."

The above quote shows how important Heathcliff is in Catherine's life – everything would change and become "stranger" without him. This section of the text can be used to complement some ideas found earlier, specifically the ghost scene in Chapter III. Although at this point, Lockwood is staying at Wuthering Heights for a night and Catherine has been dead for years, Heathcliff is still alive so **their connection transcends both physical and metaphysical barriers.** Her existence continues to haunt Heathcliff, and she "continue[s] to be."

Our next quote contains simile to juxtapose Catherine's love for Edgar and Heathcliff.

> QUOTES :
> "My love for Linton is like the foliage in the woods: time will change it, I'm well aware, as winter changes the trees. My love for Heathcliff resembles the eternal rocks beneath: a source of little visible delight, but necessary."

Catherine's love for Edgar is overt and as easy to see as leaves on trees; however, it is fleeting and changes with the seasons. It is obvious to everyone that she does care for him to an extent, yet the depth of this 'love' is ever-changing. She loves Edgar because of what he is able to provide for her and because he is the embodiment of an ideal suitor. The imagery of "winter" implies coldness and emptiness, lacking the warmth associated with other seasons when "foliage" still grows on trees. This suggests there are times she does not feel much love, if any, towards Edgar revealing the temperamental nature of her feelings for him.

To contrast this, "the eternal rocks beneath" are an everlasting and intrinsic feature of the landscape, unchanged by centuries of passing seasons. Catherine implies her love for Heathcliff is also eternal and able to weather whatever circumstances they are placed in. Another intriguing aspect of this quote is her love described as "a source of little visible delight, but necessary." This reflects how her love for Heathcliff might be difficult to see (and not as aesthetically pleasing as "foliage"), sometimes manifesting violently, but is indispensable.

Brontë's contrast of the two types of love explore an important part of Gothic literature: passionate, emotion-fuelled romances, often plagued with tragedy and darkness. Edgar's love is light and beautiful, offering a traditional life of financial stability and material satisfaction, but Heathcliff's love provides Catherine with the opportunity to be free from societal constraints and to express all her (dark) emotions as fully as she pleases. Despite the perceived 'ugliness' of the rocks representing her love for Heathcliff, Catherine is aware that she is sacrificing a part of her freedom for this stability, hence allowing Brontë to build up to the tragic outcome of the story.

Chapter X

Soon after, Lockwood gets sick (probably due to his misadventure at Wuthering Heights) and asks Nelly to resume telling her story. He gives us a quick summary of what we've learnt about Catherine and Heathcliff so far: the "hero had run off, and never been heard of for three years; and the heroine was married." Lockwood is curious about how Heathcliff made his fortune and education in the years he was missing, but Nelly does not know.

Continuing from where she left off, Nelly explains that Edgar and his sister Isabella bend to Catherine's will, and as a result she does not showcase her violent temper. This changes on the night Heathcliff returns. He arrives at Thrushcross Grange and waits in the darkness for Nelly to walk by, ambushing her and instructing her to call Catherine down to see him. The housekeeper is almost unable to recognise him, saying that he has "altered."

Catherine, overjoyed at Heathcliff's return, requests her husband's permission for Heathcliff to join her, Edgar, and Isabella in the parlour. Reluctantly, Edgar agrees and Heathcliff enters, sitting across from Catherine. Heathcliff appears a "tall, athletic, well-formed man; beside whom [Edgar] seemed quite slender and youth-like." Catherine exclaims that Heathcliff does not deserve such a warm welcome for leaving her so abruptly. He counters by telling her that he put himself through the past few years for her sake, and that he originally returned to seek vengeance on Hindley and then end his life to escape the law. However, her kind reception has put an end to his **nefarious** plans. After a short and strained dinner, Heathcliff returns to Wuthering Heights upon Hindley's invitation to everyone's surprise.

Nefarious: immoral, wicked; associated with crime.

That night, Catherine wakes Nelly to speak to her because Edgar was "sulky" hearing her gush about Heathcliff. Nelly advises her to be grateful for her husband's love and to avoid discussing Heathcliff in front of him, but Catherine insists the two men must become friends. She explains to Nelly that Heathcliff arrived at Wuthering Heights and bested Hindley in a card game (Hindley has a gambling problem). He is willing to pay a good amount of money to live under Hindley's roof solely because he wants to be within walking distance of Thrushcross Grange.

With a renewed sense of joy, Catherine decides to apologise to Edgar and the results are visible by the lack of his sullen behaviour in the morning. He even allows Catherine and Isabella to visit Wuthering Heights that afternoon. As time passes, Heathcliff's visits to Thrushcross Grange become regular and expected events, and Isabella develops a romantic interest in the visitor for which there was "no **reciprocation** of sentiment." This upsets Edgar as he is sure Heathcliff's motives are still malicious, despite his changed exterior. He is afraid that due to the lack of a male heir, his property may fall into Heathcliff's hands if he marries Isabella.

Reciprocation: to return in the same or similar way.

One morning at breakfast, Isabella gets angry at Catherine for dismissing her whenever Heathcliff is around, claiming that he would love her if he was able to spend more time with her. In response, Catherine scolds her and provides a vivid and negative description of Heathcliff's character, stating that he "couldn't love a Linton" and would "crush [Isabella] like a sparrow's egg."

When Catherine leaves the room in anger, Isabella turns to Nelly for support, only to be further dissuaded from pursuing Heathcliff. Nelly says that she met Joseph in the town recently, and he told her that Old Mr Earnshaw's gold "runs into [Heathcliff's] pocket," as every night he and Hindley stay up drinking and gambling, digging Hindley into massive debt.

The next day, while Edgar is out, Heathcliff comes over. Catherine exposes Isabella's crush with "**feigned** playfulness" to Heathcliff. When Isabella attempts to run away, Catherine grabs her to keep her in place.

Feign: pretend, insincere.

Heathcliff seems indifferent to the entire ordeal, and Isabella sets herself free by scratching Catherine's arms. Once she is gone, Heathcliff assumes that Catherine was joking, but she assures him she was telling the truth. He is silent for a minute but then he asks an important question – if Isabella is the heir to the Linton's estate. Catherine affirms this, until Edgar has a male heir, and they quickly dismiss the topic; however, Nelly is sure Heathcliff thought about it periodically during his stay. She keeps watch of him and prays that he will leave Wuthering Heights and Thrushcross Grange but foreshadows he's "waiting his time to spring and destroy."

Analysis

Heathcliff's return has sparked a range of emotions in the other characters, such as joy in Catherine, annoyance (and probably jealousy) in Edgar, love in Isabella, and a level of **trepidation** in Nelly. These negative feelings from Nelly and Edgar stem from their awareness of Heathcliff's ulterior motives. Despite claiming he has no more desire for revenge, he is still planning something as he siphons money away from Hindley. This is further evidenced by his interest in Isabella's position as heir to the Linton estate. Now that he knows Isabella likes him, Nelly suspects he will use this information to his advantage (and she is correct!).

Trepidation: apprehension or anxiety about something soon to come.

An example of Heathcliff's brutal nature, which Catherine overlooks, is his response to Isabella's scratches: "I'd wrench [Isabella's nails] off her fingers, if they ever menaced me." The overt seriousness of this threat should be of concern to Catherine as she claims to love Isabella. She is well aware of Heathcliff's flaws, as seen in the lecture she gives Isabella, but her confidence that Isabella will soon forget about him prevents her from seeing early signs of Heathcliff's plan. Additionally, **Heathcliff's quick accumulation of wealth may have been as disturbing as his dark threats for Brontë's audience** as she evinces the potential for change brought about by the Industrial Revolution.

Another issue discussed briefly in this chapter is the rivalry between Edgar and Heathcliff as both compete for Catherine's attention. Prior to Heathcliff's return, Nelly was glad to see the newlywed couple getting along well. Edgar was already deeply enamoured with Catherine, and she was beginning to care strongly for him in turn. Now that Heathcliff is back in the picture, Catherine dotes on him, and Edgar is resentful that his wife cares for another man. He is initially very cautious about the interactions between the two of them, but soon realises that nothing he does can truly keep them apart. Heathcliff, being the third party to this ordeal, is keenly aware of the disruption he is causing, but seems to take pleasure in knowing how much Catherine still cares for him.

Chapter XI

Apparition: a
ghostly figure.

One day, on her way to Gimmerton (a nearby village), Nelly passes by a stone signpost where she and Hindley used to play as children. She envisions an **apparition** of him sitting in the grass as a child and is suddenly overcome with the desire to visit him at Wuthering Heights as she is sure this is a sign of his impending death. Upon reaching Wuthering Heights, she finds Hareton who no longer recognises her and attacks her with stones. Bribing him with an orange, she learns that Heathcliff taught him to swear and dismissed his tutor and chances of an education. The boy starts to run inside to get his father, but Heathcliff comes outside instead. Seeing him, Nelly runs away.

Hearing about his treatment of Hareton, she resolves to remain wary of his behaviour around Isabella. The next time Heathcliff comes to visit Thrushcross Grange, he notices Isabella outside and approaches her. Heathcliff looks around to make sure no one is watching, but is unaware of Nelly watching everything from the other side of a window. She is horrified to see him hug Isabella and yells out in anger, drawing Catherine's attention. As Heathcliff walks into the house, Catherine tells him off for his dubious behaviour, reminding him that Edgar could cast him out for it.

Catherine asks if Isabella had approached him, and he angrily tells her that it is not her concern whom he kisses, because he is not her husband. In return Catherine tells him that he could marry Isabella if he liked her, but she is sure he does not. Carrying on in his rage, Heathcliff claims Catherine has treated him "infernally," and she will shortly see his revenge come to fruition.

Catherine is shocked by his change in character and tells him to stop causing fights between her family. She tells him that by fighting with Edgar and "deceiving" Isabella, he will have gotten sufficient revenge for her so-called ill treatment of him. After this argument, she sits sullenly by the fire and Heathcliff broods beside her. Nelly informs Edgar of what happened and encourages him to take a firm stance against Heathcliff and Catherine's friendship. Edgar enters the kitchen, where the two are fighting again, and scolds Catherine for remaining in Heathcliff's presence. Despite Heathcliff's attempts to provoke him, Edgar remains calm and orders Heathcliff to leave the house and never return.

Catherine quickly locks the door to prevent servants coming to help, telling Edgar to fight Heathcliff himself if that is what he wants. She explains that she was defending him from Heathcliff, and is offended that he would think badly of his own wife. He tries to wrestle the key from her, but she flings it into the fire. Edgar sinks into a chair, knowing that his adversary could defeat him with minimal effort. Gloating about his perceived victory, Heathcliff taunts Catherine for choosing a "milk-blooded coward" as a husband over himself. Without warning, Edgar springs up and punches Heathcliff's throat, taking him by surprise, then he walks out through the back door.

Catherine tells Heathcliff to leave, but he is eager to beat Edgar before departing. Making up a small lie, Nelly tells him Edgar is gathering workers to fight Heathcliff while he watches, even though in truth Edgar is ready to fight alongside them. Heathcliff decides to leave as he knows he will be overpowered.

Once he is gone, Catherine takes Nelly upstairs, wondering how Edgar came to hear their conversation. Eager to keep her involvement a secret, Nelly listens to her mistress in silence. Catherine wants Nelly to convince Edgar she is ill to "frighten" and manipulate him. As Heathcliff and Edgar would not bend to her will, she plans to "break their hearts by breaking [her] own."

Nelly decides not to tell Edgar of Catherine's 'illness' and eavesdrops on their quarrel. Edgar demands Catherine choose him or Heathcliff, but she stubbornly refuses to make a decision and begins to feign illness. Nelly re-enters and encourages Edgar not to be manipulated, and he leaves Catherine to sulk. Catherine refuses to eat for the next few days trying to starve herself to punish her husband, but Edgar is unaware of her behaviour, secluding himself in the library. He tries to speak to Isabella about her feelings for Heathcliff, but she is evasive. He ends this conversation by warning her if she chooses Heathcliff, it will destroy their relationship as siblings.

Analysis

This is the first time in the novel that Edgar has directly confronted Heathcliff. It is clear that Edgar loves Catherine, and he feels irritated and betrayed by her affections for Heathcliff. The final straw is when he hears of their argument and exiles Heathcliff from the estate. What ensues is a cruel **emasculation** of Edgar's character, where he is taunted for his lack of physical strength in comparison to Heathcliff. This would likely have not affected him significantly, but Catherine joins in, insulting him with an ultimatum: "attack him [or] make an apology." She goes on to insult him sarcastically after he retreats, stating that "Heathcliff would as soon lift a finger at [him] as the king would march his army against a colony of mice." This metaphor of Heathcliff as a king and Edgar as a colony of mice is both a mockery of Edgar's physical inferiority and an **inversion of their roles** in society. Edgar, as a magistrate and member of the gentry, is demeaned below an orphaned former servant. **Brontë again diminishes Edgar's power** when Heathcliff calls him a "lamb," suggesting vulnerability, meekness, and submission.

Emasculate: to provoke feelings of weakened masculinity.

Nelly points out that "he could not avert that excess of emotion: mingled anguish and humiliation overcame him completely." Failing to conceal emotion infracts upon as his characterisation as a perfect 18th century gentleman, reserved and proper. Despite often crying in his youth, as an adult he no longer has the liberty of showing such 'weakness.' Hence, the level of anguish he experienced from this argument must have been significant enough for him to forsake his usual **stoicism.**

Stoicism: a quiet endurance of difficulty or hardship.

In contrast, Heathcliff often declares his explosive anger with over-the-top outbursts. This is a key characteristic of a Byronic hero – bouts of rage, sadness, and a myriad of other negative emotions, without concealment. **Gothic literature involves many strong emotions and portrays them as raw, harsh, and oftentimes violent.** Brontë encapsulates this through Heathcliff's quickness to make violent threats, in this chapter against Edgar – "I'll crush his ribs in like a rotten hazel-nut" – furthering his characterisation as a Byronic hero.

Chapter XII

The three Lintons steer clear of each other in the passing days, with Isabella moping outside, Edgar ruminating in his study, and Catherine starving herself in her bedroom. On the third day, Catherine finally eats and begs Nelly to tell Edgar she is "dying" because she believes he does not care for her. Still certain that her mistress is pretending to be sick for attention, Nelly refuses. Catherine is so aggrieved she rips a pillow with her teeth. As she separates the feathers based on bird species, Nelly remembers this behaviour from her childhood, where Catherine would succumb to phases of delusion, and starts to worry her illness is real. Catherine then turns to a mirror and cannot recognise herself, screaming in terror at her haunting reflection.

Nelly tries to soothe her, realising that Catherine thought she was in her old bedroom at Wuthering Heights. She explains that in the days she spent locked up alone, she tried to recall the past seven years of her life but could not remember anything. This left her confused and disoriented as she remembered being 12 years old at Wuthering Heights and was now suddenly married to a stranger. She opens the window and pines after her old life, wishing to spend more time with Heathcliff.

As Nelly is trying to restrain her, Edgar walks in, surprised to see the state of his wife. Nelly tries to make excuses, saying no one could have known Catherine was ill as she had refused to see anyone for days. Edgar embraces his wife, concerned about her health, and she slowly recognises him, ceding her anger. She threatens to jump out of the window if he mentions Heathcliff and restates that she no longer cares for Edgar at all. She tells him that although her body belongs to him, her spirit belongs outside. He is furious Nelly would keep him ignorant and warns her that the next time she will be fired.

Nelly leaves the house to go into town to find Dr Kenneth. As they talk, the doctor asks about Heathcliff's visits to the Lintons. He tells Nelly about a rumour – last night Heathcliff and Isabella spent hours in the plantations behind Thrushcross Grange, and he urged her to elope with him. Remembering the sound of horses leaving when she went to get the Doctor, Nelly runs home only to find Isabella's room empty. In order to spare Edgar a "second grief," Nelly keeps Isabella's disappearance a secret as the doctor examines Catherine. He determines Catherine needs a tranquil environment and that death is unlikely.

Neither Nelly nor Edgar sleeps that night, and in the morning a maid announces she had heard that Isabella has eloped with Heathcliff. Edgar decides not to send anyone after his sister as she made her choice, and he no longer sees her as his sister; she has "disowned" him.

Analysis

This chapter serves as a vital reminder that Nelly is an unreliable narrator, recounting this story from her specific point of view without corroboration. From her perspective, her actions are correct and justified, but from Edgar's perspective they appear purposefully provocative. Her response to his (very reasonable) distress is to try to divert blame from herself. It is interesting to speculate about what this may reveal about her as a person, because she occasionally instigates trouble despite having a seemingly pure motive. An example of this is her encouragement of Edgar's involvement in Catherine and Heathcliff's argument, and her subsequent ignorance of Catherine's claims of illness. When Edgar realises Catherine is actually sick, he is upset that Nelly hid this from him, and blames her for starting the fight that supposedly caused this illness. While this does not mean she truly started the fight, it brings the reader's attention to the fact that Nelly has more influence than she lets on and may or may not be telling the story accurately.

Similarly, she was aware of Isabella's disappearance soon after it happened, and had she informed Edgar, he may have been able to stop her from making a terrible mistake. Nelly's reasoning is understandable, but the consequences of her silence prove to be extraordinarily detrimental for both Isabella's welfare and her relationship with her brother. This event parallels Heathcliff's disappearance; Nelly knew he had overheard Catherine, but her silence led to massive miscommunication. In the way she recounts her involvement to Lockwood, **Nelly presents herself as a silent observer, but the more we examine her role, we see that sometimes her lack of action is action in itself.**

As readers it is difficult to discern whether Nelly feels any guilt towards her past behaviour, as she still tries to downplay her role in the narrative, and justifies everything she does, almost as though she is trying to convince herself it was the right choice.

Chapter XIII

Catherine begins to recover under Edgar's ever-present and loving care. One morning, he brings her flowers, and she expresses a desire to be outside once again. He reminds her that a year ago, he was desperate to have her under his roof, and now he too wants her to go outside (in hopes it will make her feel better). She comments that this time the following year she will be outside (foreshadowing her death and burial), and he will reminisce about this very moment.

The mistress moves out of her sick chamber to sit in the sunshine of the parlour. Still too unwell to return upstairs she moves into the room Lockwood is currently in. In parallel to her recovery, we discover that she is pregnant with a potential heir to Edgar's estate, thereby hopefully saving it from Heathcliff's grasp.

Regarding Heathcliff and Isabella, they have been gone for two months, and she has sent Edgar one short letter in that time. It contained a brief apology and an attempt to reconcile her relationship with him, but he does not reply. A fortnight after Edgar's letter, Nelly receives a longer one addressed to her, and she brings it out to read aloud to Lockwood, having kept it ever since. In her letter, Isabella gives her regards to Catherine and Edgar, but says she will not be able to visit them.

She, having only been at Wuthering Heights for one night, was already horrified by its residents, and more so by the man she married, questioning if her new husband is "a devil." She asks Nelly to visit soon and then recounts her first impressions of her new home. Heathcliff abandoned her almost as soon as they enter the compound, and she meets Hareton inside. She tries to befriend him, but he threatens to set his dog on her. She then asks Joseph to come inside with her, but he is seemingly appalled by her presence and unwilling to comply. Next, she knocks on another door and meets a dishevelled Hindley who appears to be angrily awaiting Heathcliff.

Isabella notes that the house has become a filthy shell of what she remembers from her childhood, with no maids or anyone willing to help her settle in. Unable to hold in her sorrow, she begins to cry, drawing Hindley's attention. He tells her to go to Heathcliff's room and lock herself in there, as he has an irresistible urge to kill Heathcliff at night. He brings out his gun to threaten her, and she briefly thinks about how powerful she would be with such a weapon.

Questioning Hindley about why he hates her husband, she learns that Heathcliff has won all of Hindley's money through gambling. Isabella leaves Hindley and finds Joseph cooking porridge by dipping his hand into it (gross!). She offers to do it herself but is not very good at cooking. While she attempts this, Hareton begins to drink milk straight from the pitcher. She tells him to use a mug, which offends Joseph as he believes she is being "**conceited.**"

Conceited: vain, narcissistic.

She resolves to eat away from them, and Joseph shows her Heathcliff's chambers, telling her there is nowhere else for her to go but in there or with the servants. Distraught by her new lifestyle, she sits on the staircase and cries, flinging her food to the floor. That night, she sleeps on a chair, only to be woken by Heathcliff and told to come into their shared room. He informs her that she will never have her own space here. His abuse is made clear, and Isabella describes him as "ingenious and unresting in seeking to gain [her] **abhorrence**!" She learns that he blames Edgar for Catherine's illness and plans to use her as a "proxy" for his punishment. Isabella finishes her letter by reminding Nelly to keep all of this a secret from Edgar and Catherine, begging her to come visit as soon as possible.

Abhorrence: hatred marked by revulsion and disgust.

Analysis

Brontë presents the stark contrast between life at Wuthering Heights and Thrushcross Grange through Isabella's experience. In doing so, she also depicts the **dilapidation** and decline of the once majestic property. She describes the floors as having turned "uniform grey" from their elegant white, and the "once brilliant pewter-dishes" are now obscured by "tarnish and dust." In comparison, Thrushcross Grange is "delightful," clean, and well-maintained by the servants and maids employed by Edgar. The depiction of Wuthering Heights as "inhospitable" and sullied by Heathcliff's presence is significant in alluding to his true and evil presence.

Dilapidation: a process or state of deterioration due to neglect or disuse.

Both houses in many ways reflect their owners and residents. Mirroring Heathcliff's tumultuous and vengeful nature, Wuthering Heights is full of chaos and contempt. The decline in the cleanliness of the property can also be interpreted as a reflection of the corruption taking over Heathcliff's body and soul. The deeper his desire for revenge, the worse the house becomes. Meanwhile, Thrushcross Grange remains **immaculate** despite internal disturbances. This mimics Edgar's ability to stay calm and restrain himself and his emotions in the face of difficulty. He always keeps up a dignified exterior no matter what may be plaguing his private life.

Immaculate: pristine; perfectly clean or maintained.

Additionally, **Brontë highlights Isabella's powerlessness and fear by her longing for a weapon** to protect herself. In the 18th century, women had to negotiate and were commonly trapped by the power dynamics of marriage. Isabella's attachment to Heathcliff further disarms her as she has moved down the rungs of social hierarchy by marrying below her class.

Chapter XIV

After reading the letter, Nelly asks Edgar for a message of forgiveness to give Isabella when she visits her, but he refuses. He states that she does not need to be forgiven, as he is "not *angry*, but [...] *sorry* to have lost her."

That afternoon, Nelly visits Isabella, saddened to see that the girl is blending in with her dismal surroundings and the "pervading spirit of neglect," soaking up the misery of the household. Heathcliff greets her cordially, appearing happier than ever, and asks that she give Isabella any letters she may have in his presence, claiming that the couple do not have secrets from one another.

Heathcliff implores Nelly for information about Catherine's health, and the housekeeper warns him to keep his distance from the Linton family. She cautions him that another argument between himself and Edgar could kill Catherine altogether, but he is adamant that he must see her. He goes on to tell Nelly that if he were in Edgar's place, and Edgar in his, he would never stop Catherine from seeing the other man until she decided so for herself. When she did though, he would certainly have "torn his heart out, and drunk his blood."

Nelly tries to convince Heathcliff that Catherine has almost forgotten him, but he refutes the possibility. This launches Heathcliff into a long monologue about how closely his and Catherine's spirits are entangled, and how her love for him is far deeper than any she may hold for Edgar: "for every thought she spends on Linton she spends a thousand on me!" This angers Isabella and she stands up for her brother.

In return Heathcliff reminds her that her brother has abandoned her and that he is all she has left now. He also tells Nelly about how desperately the young lady had tried to please him following their marriage, revealing that it took "a positive labour of **Hercules**" to rid her of her delusions that he was a "hero of romance."

Hercules: a hero in Greek mythology famous for his 12 labours, a series of impossibly difficult tasks.

He tells Nelly to inform Edgar of Isabella's suffering, gloating that he is careful to abuse her "within the limits of the law" so that she cannot file for divorce. Nelly tells Isabella to leave Wuthering Heights and escape Heathcliff, but the girl has already tried and failed. She reminds Nelly to keep her suffering a secret from her family because Heathcliff is simply using her as a tool to hurt her brother. Finally, Heathcliff casts her out of the room to speak to Nelly in private.

He tells Nelly that he will wait in the garden every night for an opportunity to sneak inside to see Catherine. He does not mean to cause Catherine harm, but he only wants to talk to her, and if Nelly is not willing to help him he threatens take matters into his own hands and will break in. Heathcliff refuses to let Nelly leave until she agrees to help him.

Presently, Nelly fears helping Heathcliff was "wrong, though expedient," and she stands by her choice as an attempt to prevent further arguments. Dr Kenneth arrives to treat Lockwood, and Nelly leaves Lockwood thinking about young Cathy Heathcliff and whether she would behave the same way as her mother if he fell in love with her.

Analysis

Nelly's firsthand account of Isabella's married life is a jarring comparison to the devotion and care present in Edgar's. Heathcliff's behaviour follows clear patterns of domestic abuse including undermining her sense of worth, verbal abuse (calling her a "slut"), and attempts to intercept her private correspondence. Divorce was incredibly rare if not impossible during this time period, especially for women seeking to initiate the process. Even so, Heathcliff is careful to avoid "giving her the slightest right to claim a separation." Although Nelly wishes she could do more to help Isabella, she does not take any action to save her from Heathcliff's violence. She also succumbs to Heathcliff's demands to pass a note on to Catherine, thereby going behind her master's back. Her betrayal bothers her, but she hopes it will prevent further confrontation between the two men.

This chapter is therefore plagued with a sense of helplessness felt by both Nelly and Isabella. It shows how far Heathcliff is willing to go to get what he wants and reveals his shamelessly evil treatment of his wife. Furthermore, Isabella's assimilation to her dreary and desolate surroundings is a subtle reminder of when Edgar deemed Heathcliff "a moral poison that would contaminate the most virtuous" in Chapter XI. This "poison" has injected itself into her life and by hiding it from her brother, she hopes to prevent it from reaching him too.

Chapter XV

In 1801, a week has passed and Lockwood is recovering from his illness. Having heard the rest of the story from Nelly, he believes she is "a very fair narrator" and repeats a condensed version to us.

Four days after her visit to Wuthering Heights, Nelly gives Heathcliff's letter to Catherine and she leaves the door open for him to enter the house while everyone else is at church. He comes to Catherine's room and embraces her, knowing deep in his heart that she would die soon. They hug and kiss each other for some time before Catherine blames both him and Edgar for her broken heart (which we know from chapter XI is partly self-destruction) and imminent death.

She asks if he will forget about her once she is gone and hopes that he will suffer as she has done. He says her words will haunt him once she is dead, and that he would never forget her: "I could as soon forget you as my existence!" Refusing to show her his overwhelming emotions, Heathcliff walks to the fireplace and Catherine declares to him and Nelly that soon she will be "incomparably beyond and above," free to roam the moors in death. She beckons him closer and stands up to go to him. As she is still weak, she collapses into his arms, and he sits back on a chair, holding her close. She is motionless for a moment and Nelly is worried, but Heathcliff guards her "like a mad dog [...] with greedy jealousy" (there's that canine imagery again!). He cries and calls her cruel for marrying Edgar, and that it is her own fault she is dying. They both weep in each other's arms.

Edgar is seen coming back from church. Heathcliff tries to pull away, promising to return at night but Catherine holds onto him, refusing to let him go. Catherine says that Edgar will let him stay or else she will die, and while they are talking, the man in question comes up the stairs. Heathcliff remains in the chair, holding Catherine, and Nelly cries out to get Edgar's attention. Catherine has gone still by the time he enters the room. He is ready to attack Heathcliff, but he is persuaded to help his wife first.

Catherine returns to consciousness while Heathcliff waits in the parlour, but when she wakes up, she does not recognise anyone or anything. While Edgar is distracted, Nelly bids Heathcliff to leave the house and he agrees to wait in the garden until morning so that she can update him on Catherine.

Analysis

Brontë uses powerful imagery to reinforce the strength of Heathcliff and Catherine's relationship. Three specific quotes highlight how their connection can transcend the barriers of life and death, overpowering forces as strong as God and Satan.

> QUOTES :
> "I only wish us never to be parted: and should a word of mine distress you hereafter, think I feel the same distress underground."

This quote from Catherine follows Heathcliff's argument. He believes she will be at peace while he is suffering above ground (alive), but she knows she will "feel the same distress underground" (in death). This indicates their relationship (and suffering) will not hindered by her death, persisting beyond the realm of the living.

> QUOTES :
> "Because misery and degradation, and death, and nothing that God or Satan could inflict would have parted us, *you,* of your own will, did it"

This quote from Heathcliff brings omniscient and omnipotent beings (God and Satan) into the equation. He believes their bond is so strong that such forces are unable to part them, and directly blames Catherine for separating them by choosing Edgar.

Gothic and Romantic literature explore the power of human connection in relation to religion, as the Age of Enlightenment brought traditions into question. This statement echoes some humanist sentiments by hinting Heathcliff and Catherine's love can topple even powerful deities; however, it can also be interpreted as a hyperbole designed to show the intensity of their relationship.

QUOTES :

"What kind of living will it be when you – oh, God! would *you* like to live with your soul in the grave?"

This rhetorical question frames Catherine as Heathcliff's soul. It can be linked to the quote from Chapter IX where Catherine tells Nelly "whatever our souls are made of, his and mine are the same," reiterating that Catherine feels so close to Heathcliff that it is like they share a soul.

Chapter XVI

Catherine gives birth prematurely to her daughter Cathy at midnight and passes away two hours later, leaving Edgar distraught. He has now lost his wife and does not have a male heir to inherit his property, leaving it to Isabella (and hence Heathcliff) upon his death. (Old Mr Linton's will stated that Edgar inherit, then his sons and so on. Since Edgar had no sons, Isabella is next in line to inherit after Edgar's death.)

Young Cathy spends the first few hours of her life neglected while everyone is busy grieving the loss of her mother. The next morning Nelly finds Edgar asleep beside the body with an anguished expression on his face, while Catherine's bore an expression of "perfect peace." Later, Nelly steps outside to find Heathcliff, but he seems aware of the news before she can tell him. He snaps at her to stop crying because Catherine wouldn't want her tears. Little does he know that Nelly is weeping for him too out of pity.

He demands to know how exactly Catherine died but cannot ask the question without shaking. Nelly mentally chastises him for trying to hide his emotions, but tells him that Catherine died peacefully, never regaining enough consciousness to recognise or remember anyone. He cries out, begging for her spirit to "haunt" and "drive [him] mad" as he "*cannot live without [his] soul!*"

Catherine's coffin is placed in the drawing room, open until her funeral. Edgar spends his sleepless nights and days beside it, until one day he goes to rest for a few hours. Nelly leaves a window open for Heathcliff, who has been lurking outside, to allow him to say goodbye and he bids his "idol one final adieu." Afterwards, the only evidence of his presence is a small lock of light-coloured hair (probably Edgar's) on the floor. The housekeeper opens the locket around Catherine's neck, finding Heathcliff's black hair there instead. She twists them together in a symbolic gesture (that will see a part of both men buried with her) and puts it back.

Hindley never responds to his invitation to view his sister's body, and Isabella is not contacted at all. To everyone's surprise, Catherine is not buried in the chapel with the Lintons or in the tombs outside with the Earnshaws, but instead in a "corner of the kirkyard, where the wall is so low that heath [...] climbed over it from the moor." Nelly adds the detail that Edgar is buried there now too. This symbolic and physical closeness, Heathcliff through his namesake plant (and later his burial) and Edgar in burial, poignantly marks the end of the tale about Catherine's life.

Analysis

This chapter deals with grief in a very raw and emotional fashion. **Brontë shows how different characters seek solace from the pain of bereavement in different ways.** Edgar's grief is silent and ever-present as he spends every waking minute with Catherine's body as "a sleepless guardian." Nelly seeks solace by thinking of Catherine's newfound freedom in eternal life, which she thinks is "endless and shadowless hereafter." This brings her great comfort during this difficult time, even though she occasionally wonders whether a soul as tumultuous as Catherine's will make it to heaven.

To contrast these peaceful methods of grieving, Brontë presents Heathcliff's as equally ever-present as Edgar's but more violent and destructive in line with his characterisation as a Byronic hero. When Nelly sees Heathcliff he bangs his head against a tree trunk and she notices "splashes of blood about the bark of the tree," indicating he had done this periodically and with force enough to draw blood. She perceives his grief as wild and animalistic, describing his weeping as "howl[ing], not like a man, but like a savage beast being goaded to death with knives and spears." Furthermore, rather than wishing for peace for Catherine's soul, he hopes she is tormented by the same pain that plagues him for as long as he lives.

Brontë also had to deal with grief as the deaths of several of her family members, and the contrast of way loss is felt by her characters may reflect her own experiences with mourning.

Chapter XVII

The next few weeks are full of wintry weather that reflects the mood of everyone at Thrushcross Grange. Edgar has retreated to his room and Nelly converts the parlour into a nursery for the new baby. One morning, while she is attending to the baby, a giddy visitor bursts into the house. At first Nelly is horrified that someone would have the audacity to be happy at such a terrible time, but then she realises the visitor is none other than Isabella who is soaked by the snow and injured from running all the way from Wuthering Heights.

She asks Nelly to organise a carriage to take her to Gimmerton, and then changes out of her wet garments into dry ones. Once everything is sorted out, Isabella throws her wedding ring into the fire and tells Nelly that she must leave soon in case Heathcliff comes after her. She does not want to see Edgar, and she does not want Heathcliff's presence to disturb her brother's grief, and thus must be on her way within an hour.

Nelly enquires where she plans to go. While Isabella would love to stay at Thrushcross Grange to cheer up her brother and take care of her niece, she is sure Heathcliff would "resolve on poisoning [their] comfort" if she remained with them. She initially wished Heathcliff would kill her so she could escape her torment, but now she hopes he will kill himself. His "devilish nature" has "extinguished her love" entirely. After his abuse and "murderous" rage, she finally has the opportunity to run away.

She tells Nelly that Hindley had sobered up to attend the funeral but when the time came he sat by the fire and drank himself to oblivion. Heathcliff had been missing from the household for the past week (we know from the previous chapter that he was loitering outside the Grange).

The previous night, Heathcliff returns earlier than expected from the Grange due to a storm. Hindley locks him out and takes out his gun, suggesting that he and Isabella work together to kill Heathcliff. He tells her to sit still and be quiet while he saves her from her husband's violence and ensures justice for Hareton. Isabella, of the opinion that "treachery and violence are spears pointed at both ends," shouts a warning to Heathcliff before Hindley can put his plan into action. As much as she wants him dead, she realises she cannot be a part of a cold-blooded murder. Heathcliff tells her to open the kitchen door instead, and she taunts him by telling him to return to Catherine's grave like a "faithful dog." Hindley tries to shoot through the window, but Heathcliff snatches it and slashes Hindley's arm with the knife attached to the gun. Breaking the window with a rock, Heathcliff get in and beats Hindley, before eventually relenting and bandaging the knife wound.

Just before noon the next day, Isabella dines alone, watching Hindley (still alive) and Heathcliff both sulk. She comments that the risk of offending Catherine used to hold Heathcliff back from inflicting "bodily harm" on Hindley and now she is gone. She muses aloud she is dead because Heathcliff disturbed their peace, and then laughs at him as he cries by the fire. She continues to goad Heathcliff until he throws a knife at her in rage and she runs (to Thrushcross Grange) before he can reach her.

Finished with her story, she kisses Edgar and Catherine's portraits and steps into the carriage, never to return. Once settled in the "south, near London," she and Edgar correspond through letters. Shortly after, Isabella gives birth to Heathcliff's son whom she names Linton. From the very beginning, she reports him to be a sickly child.

Heathcliff finds out where she lives, but surprisingly does not go after her, even after discovering he has a son. He tells Nelly that when he wants the boy, he will "have it." (That time comes thirteen years later, when Isabella passes away.)

The day after Isabella's surprise visit, Nelly tells Edgar that his sister has run away from her husband. He is glad, but still consumed with grief. He abandons his role as the local magistrate, stops attending church, and only goes out for walks along the moors or to Catherine's grave. As time passes, although he does not resume his social life, he begins to heal from his pain and remember his wife with joy. He dotes on his young daughter, seeing her as an extension of her mother.

Nelly wonders why Edgar and Hindley both went down such different paths when they were affected by similar circumstances. Frances' death led Hindley to spiral into despair, alcohol, and gambling, polluting his love for his son. However, Edgar found comfort in God, devoting himself to giving his daughter the best life possible.

A mere six months after his sister's death, Hindley dies from alcohol poisoning. Dr Kenneth delivers the news to Thrushcross Grange. Hindley was like a brother to Nelly; they grew up together and were both born in the same year, making him only 27 years old when he died. She suspects a level of foul play in his death, and pleads with Edgar to let her attend to his last rites at Wuthering Heights.

She also tries to convince Edgar to inquire about his brother-in-law's property and Hareton's wellbeing, but he directs her to contact his lawyer as he is not in a state to handle such affairs. Edgar's lawyer was also Hindley's lawyer, and he tells Nelly Hindley mortgaged Wuthering Heights to fund his drinking and gambling addictions leaving Hareton deeply in debt. Heathcliff now owns Wuthering Heights because he was the lender from whom Hindley borrowed money.

Jospeh is relieved that Nelly has come to look after the funeral preparations. Heathcliff says Hindley should be buried without ceremony; however, Nelly insists on a proper burial. Nelly also insists Edgar will take in Hareton (since he is Catherine's nephew), but Heathcliff threatens to take his own son from Isabella unless they leave Hareton in his care, thus Hareton grows up living as a servant at Wuthering Heights ignorant of what he could've had.

Analysis

An overarching theme of this chapter (and throughout the text) is revenge. Isabella abstains from it during her escape and Heathcliff enacts it on the next generation after Hindley's death.

When Isabella warns Heathcliff about Hindley's plan to kill him, it makes the reader question her motives, as she has expressed on numerous occasions the desire to kill her husband. It seems paradoxical that when presented with the opportunity, she does not take it. Isabella is aware that revenge is "pointed at both ends" and one risks harming themselves in the act of it. In contrast, Heathcliff pursues revenge with narrow-minded focus, a motivator for every course of action, consuming him and resulting in the destruction and misery of those around him.

Prior to Isabella's arrival at Wuthering Heights, we know little of Hindley as Nelly (the narrator) had no contact with him. However, with the addition of Isabella's perspective, we can see the overwhelming anger and sadness driving his overindulgence in drinking and gambling. The reader then becomes aware that his hatred for Heathcliff is no longer based on his skin colour, or any other petty childhood disagreements, but instead it is rooted in how Heathcliff is ruining both his and Hareton's lives. Despite almost killing him as a child and appearing to alternate between cherishing and abhorring his son, Hindley still cares deeply for Hareton. Part of the reason he wants Heathcliff dead is to seek "justice" for Hareton, but he is foiled in his attempt to shoot Heathcliff, and dies shortly after.

With Hindley gone, Heathcliff decides to raise the boy and declares "we'll see if one tree won't grow as crooked as another, with the same wind to twist it!" Hence, the story has come full circle. Hindley had reduced Heathcliff to the level of a servant and now that he is dead, Heathcliff (as the "wind") plans to treat ("twist") Hareton in a similar fashion, thereby taking his malice for the boy's father out on him.

Chapter XVIII

The next 12 years are among the best of Nelly's life as she watches Cathy grow up. She is a gentle and tender child, but also a little spoilt due to the care and attention of her father. Edgar has made her education his duty, and "she learned rapidly and eagerly." To keep her safe, Cathy was not allowed out of the gardens unless accompanied. She knows nothing of Heathcliff or Wuthering Heights, although she occasionally wonders what lies beyond the hills.

Nelly changes the subject to Isabella's death, attributing it to a sort of fever (similar to what kills Edgar a few years later). When she fell ill, Isabella sent Edgar a letter asking him to visit her so that she may see him one last time and transfer her son, Linton, safely into his hands. Edgar is gone for three weeks, leaving Cathy under Nelly's care with the instructions that she is not to leave the border of the property unaccompanied. For the first few days, Cathy is quiet and well-behaved, but after that she becomes restless, so Nelly sends her on imaginary adventures to ride her pony across the grounds.

One day Cathy asks for extra food because she is taking some of her dogs with her, pretending to be an "Arabian merchant, going to cross the Desert" and Nelly obliges, certain Cathy won't go too far. When it is time for tea, the girl does not return and servants set out to find her. Nelly learns that she set out across the moors to explore Penistone Crags, a rock formation that she has admired for years.

Terrified that she is injured, or even dead, Nelly journeys in that direction, stopping at Wuthering Heights when she sees one of the dogs in the yard. The new housekeeper welcomes her and reassures her that Cathy is safe and that Heathcliff and Joseph are both out. When she enters, Cathy is talking animatedly to Hareton who is now 18 years old.

She scolds Cathy, urging her to put on her hat and leave before dark. Nelly is frustrated when she doesn't listen; in her irritation, she blurts out that if the girl knew who owned the house she would want to leave as quickly as possible. Cathy believes the house belongs to Hareton's father, but he says no. Then assuming he is a servant she orders him to fetch her pony, outraged that he does not treat her with the respect she is used to.

She then instructs the housekeeper to get her pony and dogs. The housekeeper reminds her to be civil and tells her that Hareton is her cousin. Cathy is distraught to hear she is related to the "clown" Hareton, claiming that her father has gone to London to fetch her cousin who she calls a "gentleman's son." Despite her (insulting) reaction, Hareton takes pity on her, bringing her pony out. Nelly feels uncomfortable for two reasons – the first being that Cathy now knows she is related to Hareton and will have many questions for Edgar, and the second that Heathcliff's household knows Linton is coming to Thrushcross Grange.

While Hareton tends to the animals, Nelly thinks about his upbringing. It upsets her to know that Heathcliff has channelled his efforts into stunting the boy's intellectual and social growth, encouraging the development of his bad habits and vices. She also suspects Joseph never took any action to rectify this, instead surmising Heathcliff will pay for his wrongdoings after he dies. This is mostly speculation though, Nelly tells Lockwood, as she has only heard rumours about the happenings of Wuthering Heights over those 12 years. The only certain fact is that Heathcliff does not interact with anyone often and prefers solitude.

They return home and Nelly carefully tells Cathy that Edgar does not get along with the family living at Wuthering Heights, and that he will be very upset to hear she disobeyed his instructions. She also mentions that if he finds out about her negligence, Edgar may fire her. Since Cathy cannot bear the thought of losing Nelly she promises not to tell her father.

Analysis

Cathy Linton is introduced as both a sweet and spoilt child. She is innocent and naïve, untainted by the tragedy and darkness that surrounds her. However, it is only due to Edgar's constant vigilance and overprotectiveness has left her ignorant and used to having her way.

Hareton and the housekeeper's refusal to follow orders shakes the Cathy's entire social foundation, as she is exposed to a world outside her sheltered childhood. It comes as a shock to her that there are those out there who do not respect her or her father.

Another interesting feature of this chapter is the **depiction of Thrushcross Grange as good and safe, and the moors as the exact opposite.** Think of that scene in The Lion King: "everything the light touches is our kingdom." Cathy is confined to her kingdom (Thrushcross Grange) and, like Simba, is forbidden from going to the "shadowy place" (Wuthering Heights and the moors). Multiple times in this chapter, Cathy is reminded to stay where it is safe and to steer clear of the temptation to explore Penistone Crags. An example of this is when Nelly tries to deter her by saying "Thrushcross Park is the finest place in the world."

Chapter XIX

A letter from Edgar announces his return with his nephew and informs us that Isabella is dead. Cathy anticipates the arrival of "her 'real' cousin" and greets her father ecstatically when he steps out from the carriage. Nelly studies Linton, who is sleeping inside, describing him as a "pale, delicate, effeminate boy." Edgar advises everyone to be careful with Linton as he is still grieving the loss of his mother, and his health is precarious. The boy cries at the smallest of inconveniences, and Cathy takes to him with a maternal affection. Edgar has hope that the company of another child his age will soon lift his spirits.

That night, Joseph comes to Thrushcross Grange. He informs Edgar that Heathcliff wants his son sent to Wuthering Heights immediately. Edgar is reluctant to agree but knowing that Heathcliff's claim to the child is stronger than his own, he relents to send the boy in the morning. He is upset that he cannot keep his promise to Isabella, to take care of her son and keep him safe from Heathcliff.

Analysis

This very short chapter gives us some insight into Cathy and Linton's characters. Cathy's upbringing has been devoid of any playmates her own age, and her excitement to meet her cousin stems from her desire to fill this social cavity. This is likely why she dotes on him and tries to "make a pet of her little cousin [...] stroking his curls, and kissing his cheek [...] like a baby." We can see she has accepted him as a relative, unlike her reaction to Hareton.

Linton's character is portrayed as weak and childish. He complains that he cannot sit on a chair and begins to cry, revealing to the reader both his poor health and entitled nature. When faced with Cathy's affection, he "dried his eyes, and lightened into faint smile," evidence of his intense need for attention and care. Being his mother's only child, it can be inferred that he was likely spoilt and greatly cared for, which is why he expects the same level of treatment in his new home.

Chapter XX

Edgar tells Nelly to take Linton to Wuthering Heights early in the morning, to keep his new residence a secret from Cathy. He does not want her to visit him. All she will know is that Linton's father has sent for him, and he had to go immediately. As Nelly rouses Linton, he asks many questions about why his mother never mentioned his father, and how he will learn to love a man he never knew existed. Nelly does her best to keep his spirits high, even though it involves telling him some lies about why his parents separated.

The boy does not want to leave, so Nelly employs Edgar's help. After bestowing him with many empty promises of visits and a romanticised picture of what his life at Wuthering Heights will be like, she finally convinces him to go. Once they reach their destination, Linton is visibly displeased by the exterior, although he holds out hope for his new family. Upon seeing him, everyone is surprised by his weak frame, and Heathcliff is immediately disgusted by his son. Linton begins to cry and Heathcliff brings him inside, inspecting him. He promises to take good care of him, starting with giving him breakfast. Heathcliff turns to Nelly, verbalising how much he abhors the boy. Even though he does not like him, he has prepared a tutor for him, and made Hareton his servant, all because the boy is Edgar's heir and Heathcliff's pathway to possession of Thrushcross Grange.

Joseph brings Linton some porridge, but he refuses to eat it. Heathcliff indulges him and tells Joseph to bring him something else. Nelly is ready to leave, but the moment the door closes, she can hear Linton begging her not to abandon him. Still, she leaves.

Analysis

Heathcliff's disdain for Linton is clear, both for his weak constitution and his resemblance to Isabella. He objectifies and dehumanises the boy, using the words "it," "thing," and "my property." Linton is a tool for Heathcliff's revenge and plot to secure Thrushcross Grange as his own. We know he succeeds as Mr Lockwood is now his tenant. This may be a little confusing, but it hinges on the fact that Edgar has no sons (refer to page 8).

Since Old Mr Linton's will dictates that the property would fall to Isabella in such a case, the next natural heir would be Isabella's son, Linton. Heathcliff knows that Linton will not live a long life, but he needs him to outlive Edgar to inherit the property. Once both Linton and Edgar are dead, the property will belong to Linton's closest male relative – that being Heathcliff, as Linton's father. This fixation on material inheritance, and not any sense of parental love or responsibility, is why he wants his son to stay with him.

Chapter XXI

Cathy is inconsolable when she finds her cousin gone but, with time, she falls back into her old lifestyle. In town, Nelly meets the housekeeper of Wuthering Heights and enquires about the boy. He is still ill and Heathcliff cannot stand being in the same room as him. The boy is paranoid about everything, such as an open window letting in the "killing" cold, or Joseph's pipe of "poison."

Edgar still cares a great deal for the boy and asks Nelly to update him with anything she finds out. However, he cannot do anything to help the boy because of the close eye Heathcliff keeps on him. Nelly also tells us that the housekeeper who gave her this information leaves Wuthering Heights two years later and is replaced by Zillah.

Life continues in this fashion until Cathy's 16th birthday, when she asks Nelly to take her on a walk through the moors to see some birds' nests. She keeps walking, Nelly becomes suspicious as they near Wuthering Heights. Heathcliff finds her poking around in search of the birds' eggs and begins to question her. She tells him that she is Edgar's daughter and recognises Hareton as he approaches. Nelly finally catches up and prompts her to return to Thrushcross Grange.

Heathcliff politely invites them in, piquing Cathy's curiosity by telling her that she knows his son. Despite Nelly's warnings, Cathy enters the house and Heathcliff grabs Nelly, forcing her inside as well. He divulges to Nelly his plan: "that the two cousins may fall in love, and get married" to avoid future property disputes.

Heathcliff introduces Cathy to Linton who has grown tall and is looking a little healthier. The two cousins rejoice in meeting each other and Cathy, realising that Heathcliff is her uncle, asks why he never visits Thrushcross Grange. He tells her that he and Edgar has a falling out, and to keep her visits to Wuthering Heights a secret if she wants to continue seeing her cousin.

She suggests that Linton visit her at her house, but the boy is "vapid" and reluctant due to his poor health, drawing some suppressed anger from Heathcliff. He turns to Nelly, telling her that he wishes his son could be like Hareton and he'd would "have loved the lad had he been some one else." Heathcliff tries to get Linton to take Cathy outside, but he is more content to sit by the fire. Instead, he calls Hareton to entertain Cathy.

Heathcliff is glad in making Hareton suffer as he did in his own childhood and promises that there will be worse to come. Hareton does not even realise his inflicted inferiority and is loyal despite experiencing mistreatment. Linton sits uneasily by the fire, regretting his decision to let Cathy go outside without him and, upon Heathcliff's insistence, he follows his cousins outside.

He joins them and begins to tease Hareton for his illiteracy. Cathy and Linton laugh at Hareton and take pleasure at his humiliation as he walks away. Nelly is ashamed of the young man's behaviour and suddenly loses some of the pity she felt for him.

On the way home that afternoon, Nelly tries to tell Cathy about the residents of Wuthering Heights, but she does not want to hear about it, convinced that her uncle is a good man. She tells Edgar all about her visit the next day, asking him why he let his 'petty' fight with Heathcliff separate her from her cousin. Edgar tells her that Heathcliff has an "evil disposition" but she is convinced otherwise from his "cordial" manner, smiles, and "softened" voice. Reluctantly, Edgar recounts how Heathcliff came into possession of Wuthering Heights and how he had a hand to play in her mother's death. Appalled by these revelations, Cathy agrees to obey her father.

That night, Nelly finds her crying in her bedroom, worried that Linton will wait for her arrival in vain as she is not allowed to go. She wants to write a letter to Linton to explain her predicament, but Nelly stops her. However, a few weeks later, Nelly learns she was successful in sending not just one but a stack of letters.

Cathy begins to act more secretively, hiding her books and locking her drawers when Nelly is around. One night, Nelly opens her locked drawer and discovers love letters from Linton. She removes them, deeming them "very worthless trash," and intercepts the dairymaid who has been carrying the letters, instructing him to stop facilitating their correspondence. When Cathy discovers her empty drawer she is heartbroken. She promises Nelly that she will stop writing to her cousin if she can get her letters back. Nelly reprimands her, reminding her that she barely knows the boy and decides to show Edgar the letters. Cathy begs her to burn the letters instead, and she agrees on the condition that the two teenagers cease their correspondence. Nelly replies to Linton's next letter, informing him that Cathy "will not receive them" anymore.

Analysis

This chapter reveals the extent of Heathcliff's manipulative nature – he is willing to interfere with the lives of the younger generation for his own benefit. It also sheds some light on his relationship with his son, which has been the subject of much speculation for the past few years. We learn that Heathcliff holds some level of respect for Hareton, despite his resentment for him as Hindley's son. Hareton is handsome, physically strong, and has the capacity for great intelligence. Meanwhile, Heathcliff's own son Linton is weak, both physically and in character. He describes Hareton as "gold put to the use of paving-stones" and Linton as "tin polished to ape a service of silver." **Brontë uses this elemental association to polarise the boys** by delineating their value – "gold" (Hareton) and "tin" (Linton) – against their different social classes ("paving-stones" and "silver").

Furthermore, Heathcliff's manipulation of Cathy and Linton can be seen when he tries to make them walk together outside. He barely supresses his contempt for Linton who is too "absorbed in drying his own feet" to follow his father's plans to obtain Thrushcross Grange. This continues as Heathcliff encourages Cathy to visit Linton in secret, vilifying Edgar and boosting his own standing in the girl's eyes.

As we saw prior and during to his marriage with Isabella, Heathcliff uses a charming façade to ingratiate himself before revealing his true personality (which Cathy will see later in the text). This is not unlike real domestic violence situations.

Chapter XXII

Summer comes and goes, and Edgar catches a terrible cold that leaves him incapacitated for the whole winter. Cathy has become sadder since her romance was nipped in the bud. Nelly reluctantly accompanies Cathy for a walk, knowing it is going to rain, as an attempt to distract her from her father's declining health. When she sees Cathy crying, she learns that the girl is afraid of both Nelly and Edgar dying and leaving her alone. Nelly comforts her by telling her that they are still young, and that her father only has a cold, "nothing worse." Cathy brings up Isabella's death, but Nelly tells her that her aunt died because she had less to live for and no one to care for her.

Nelly takes this opportunity to tell Cathy not to do anything that could potentially upset her father, such as loving Linton, the son of "a person who would be glad to have [Edgar] in his grave." Cathy says she cares for "nothing in comparison with papa" and she will not do anything to hurt him.

Her spirits lightened, they continue their walk and she happily up to sit on the wall at the edge of the property. Her hat falls over to the other side, so she climbs down to get it, but cannot come back up. Nelly tells her to wait while she tries to find someone who can open the door but before she can leave Heathcliff approaches the girl. Nelly cannot see him, but she can hear the whole conversation.

Cathy wants nothing to do with him after she hearing her father's side of the story, but he tells her that Linton is dying, hastened by her lack of affection. Nelly tries to bash the lock open with a rock, imploring the girl not to believe a word of what he says. He appeals to her compassion by asking her to imagine the roles reversed, and her father was appealing to Linton to help save her. The lock gives way and Nelly bursts out, grabbing Cathy by the arm to bring her inside. Heathcliff leaves with the parting words – there is no one to care for Linton at Wuthering Heights, and he "pines for kindness, as well as love." To sweeten his appeal, he promises that he will not be home all week allowing her the opportunity to visit.

They return to Thrushcross Grange in a hurry as the rain starts falling. Edgar is asleep. Cathy is torn, desperate to put Linton at ease but also to obey her father. So, to make her feel better, she and Nelly set out for Wuthering Heights the next day, Nelly of the impression that Linton's attitude will deter the girl from believing Heathcliff's lies.

Analysis

As the final part of Heathcliff's plan is set into action, Cathy's compassion and naïveté will bring about her downfall. He continues to play the part of a polite uncle and a concerned father in front of her, never letting her see his true nature, thereby casting doubt upon the credibility of Edgar's account.

Aside from this, the chapter also characterises Cathy as a caring daughter and depicts her first struggle with concept of death. A lone bluebell is described by the girl as "melancholy," imprinting her own feelings on the flower. The Brontë sisters often employed flowers in their creative works, weaving in a subtler meaning through **floriography.** Emily and Anne Brontë both wrote poems titled *The Bluebell,* a flower that signifies constancy and everlasting love, as well as death and grief. In her poem, **Brontë links the flower to a longing for home, an additional meaning that becomes apparent after the event of Cathy's marriage.**

Floriography: meaning attributed to different types of flowers, often used to convey a message or emotion.

We see Cathy's unconditional love and compassion for her father when she says: "I pray every night that I may live after him; because I would rather be miserable than that he should be: that proves I love him better than myself." This selfless notion of outliving her father so that he does not have to suffer the pain of her death reveals that she is willing to go through pain to protect him from experiencing the same.

Chapter XXIII

True to his word, Heathcliff is not home when they arrive. Joseph is sitting in the kitchen, ignoring Linton's angry orders to add more kindling to his dying fire. He mistakes Nelly and Cathy's footsteps for Joseph and yells at them before quickly correcting himself. Pitying his sickly form, Nelly adds more coal to the fire. He tells Cathy that she should have visited him instead of writing letters as replying "tired him dreadfully." Heathcliff had made Linton believe it was his fault Cathy did not come to visit. She tells Linton "next to papa and Ellen, I love you better than anybody living" and would visit if her father allowed her to. They begin to discuss love in the context of sibling and marital ties, devolving into an argument about their parents' marriages and ending when Cathy pushes Linton's chair, triggering a coughing fit.

The girl is remorseful and cries each time he groans in pain. He seems to enjoy this and guilts her by describing the pain: "you've hurt me so that I shall lie awake all night choking with this cough." Growing tired, he stops talking to her and she finally agrees to leave with Nelly. Cathy wants to nurse Linton but Nelly forbids her from returning.

In the following days, Nelly also falls ill and is confined to her room for three weeks. Cathy waits on her and her father dutifully. Unbeknownst to Nelly at the time, Cathy spends her evenings sneaking out to Wuthering Heights to visit her cousin.

Analysis

Linton's entitled and petulant behaviour turns to manipulation as he blames Cathy for his predicament. He is a miserable and lonely person who knows that no one in his own household likes him (similar to Heathcliff) and as a result looks to Cathy for the love he lacks. Her caring nature makes her inclined to help Linton, and the slightest attention from him brings her joy. Cathy is also a lonely person. Despite having the company of her father and Nelly, she longs for someone her own age.

The methods the two characters employ in seeking to end their loneliness are very different. Linton makes himself out to be helpless and tricks his cousin into spending time with him. Meanwhile Cathy is honest and genuine in her care for him: "if I could only get papa's consent, I'd spend half my time with you." However, her selflessness will not be rewarded with kindness in turn and instead used by Linton for his own gain.

Chapter XXIV

As Nelly recovers, she asks Cathy to sit and read to her in the evenings and she reluctantly obliges. On the third day, she complains of a headache and retires to her chambers but when Nelly goes to check on her, she is not there. The servants have not seen her, and Nelly waits in the girl's bedroom for her to return.

Pressured by Nelly, she confesses she has been visiting Wuthering Heights regularly during these past few weeks. At first, she enjoyed her trips as she would sit and talk happily with Linton, but soon she realised he was not fond of playing games or moving around much, which upset her. On her third visit, she runs into Hareton who can now proudly read the letters inscribed on the house. She appears happy for him, but quickly reverts to calling him a "dunce" for being unable to read the numbers.

Nelly interjects to remind her that Hareton is also her cousin and that he would be hurt by how she and Linton bullied him, and that he was probably trying to impress her. The girl continues with her story. Linton was sick that day, so she simply read to him in front of the fire.

This peace was interrupted when Hareton cast them out, sending them to Linton's room and claiming the common space for himself and Joseph. The door was locked and Linton, with "an expression of frantic, powerless fury," began yelling that he would kill them if he was not let in. Joseph observed Linton was finally showing some similarities to his father. Linton started shrieking and coughing up blood, so Cathy went outside to find Zillah. On their return, Hareton had carried the boy upstairs and she was told to leave. She threatened Hareton by telling him she will have him thrown in prison and hanged. On her way home, he came up beside her horse to explain himself but she strikes him with her whip, sending him away.

Cathy spent the next night at home, tempted but not ready to go back. When she finally did, Zillah told her Linton was much better and led her to a clean room. Here, Linton was reading one of the books she gave him, but he was in a terrible mood and blamed her for sparking the entire incident. She skipped the next day, too insulted to return, but her boredom caused her to go once again the day after.

This time she was ready to make it her last visit but he seems to repent. Linton tells her Heathcliff calls him "worthless," and hence he has grown bitter and angry, internalising the idea that he is defective. He allows her to leave if she pleased but claims to love her and would regret showing his ill temper to her until the day he died. Taking his words for the truth, she forgives him and continued to visit every day, careful to stay in Linton's private parlour to avoid Heathcliff.

Only a few of her visits were pleasant, but she endures her cousin's "selfishness and spite" for his sake. One night she even hears Heathcliff "abusing poor Linton cruelly for his conduct" and interrupts to tell him that it is the "business of nobody but [her]." Heathcliff seems amused by this. Cathy implores Nelly to keep this a secret from Edgar. Nelly promises to think it over, and does exactly so, speaking her thoughts aloud to Edgar. The next morning, he forbids Cathy from visiting Wuthering Heights but tells her that Linton can visit her at home at any time.

Analysis

This chapter deals with Cathy's conflicting commitments to her father and to herself. In Chapter XXII, she promises never to "do an act or say a word to vex" her father, especially visiting Wuthering Heights to be with Linton. However, here she has gone back on this promise for two reasons. The first reason for this is because she feels responsible for Linton's health and wellbeing, as this is what both Linton and Heathcliff have led her to believe. The second may be due to her perceived independence and freedom to socialise. While she tries to keep these two spheres of her life separate, it is evitable that they collide due to Nelly's interference. Through Cathy and Nelly, **Brontë depicts the pernicious governance over female social engagements and courtship during a time when marriage was inextricably tied to the movement of wealth and status between families.**

Another interesting part of this section is Nelly's desperation to keep Cathy safe from the residents of Wuthering Heights. In the past, she has been privy to Catherine and Isabella's misadventures but did not take much action to prevent their errors. Occasionally, she even took an active role in causing trouble, as seen when she lets Heathcliff into the house in Chapter XV. However, when it comes to young Cathy's fascination with Linton and her encounters with Heathcliff, Nelly is much more protective and vigilant. There could be many reasons for this, but perhaps the most probable is that Cathy is the last Earnshaw/Linton descendant untainted by Heathcliff's "moral poison."

Chapter XXV

Nelly pauses her story to Lockwood for a moment to reveal these events transpired a mere year ago and questions why he shows special interest in Cathy. She muses that he and Cathy may fall in love, but as much as he wants to entertain the idea, his lifestyle requires him to move around and would not suit her.

Continuing her story, we learn Edgar is gentle with Cathy after deterring her from her nightly escapades, knowing that when he is gone his words will be all that is left for her to remember. Privately, he asks Nelly about his nephew and she tells him the boy is "very delicate" and if Cathy were to marry him, "he would not be beyond her control." She reminds Edgar that he has years to vet the boy before he must worry about their marriage, though unfortunately this proves false.

He expresses that he would have no qualms about her marriage to Linton, despite the boy being Heathcliff's son, if it meant Cathy would be consoled following his passing. However, he cannot bear to abandon his daughter to Linton if he is a tool to his father. Nelly promises to look after Cathy in the unlikely event of his passing.

As spring arrives, Edgar resumes taking strolls with his daughter. Even though he is still weak and his health is not improving, she thinks it is a sign that he will heal soon. He also writes to Linton, asking him to visit Thrushcross Grange, but the boy replies that though he cannot visit (supposedly under his father's instructions) he would love to see Cathy again. Edgar, unable to accompany his daughter for a visit, declines, but asks Linton to continue their correspondence. The boy does so but Nelly surmises his letters are thoroughly edited (or written) by Heathcliff as they sound too cheerful and optimistic for his personality. Their contents long for Cathy's company – a ploy to imbue guilt in Edgar.

Eventually in June, with the influence of Cathy's requests, Edgar allows the two to meet for a walk under Nelly's supervision. He hopes Cathy will be able to keep and live at Thrushcross Grange after his passing, and her marriage to the Linton (as the heir) will ensure this. Unfortunately, no one at Thrushcross Grange is aware that Linton's health is arguably as bad as Edgar's and they will not live long.

Analysis

In Chapter XXII, we heard Cathy's thoughts and fears regarding death, and in this chapter we learn about Edgar's. Being a parent, his utmost concern is about his daughter's wellbeing and safety. In the past, he believed he would be happier on the day he died than the day he was married, and every year on the anniversary of his wife's death, he yearns to be buried with her. However, now that death is looming, his only question is: "what can I do for Cathy?"

Since Linton will inherit Thrushcross, she will likely be cast out unless she marries him. Edgar has little to no objections to the marriage, even though it would allow Heathcliff to usurp his property and steal his "last blessing." However, the mere prospect of her having a miserable marriage terrifies Edgar and he is torn about its proceedings. This level of care reveals what a devoted father he is, and how greatly he values his child's life and happiness; **his selflessness is an inversion of Heathcliff's characterisation.**

We also see of hints of Heathcliff's machinations through his "sharp watch" over Linton's correspondence. Nelly suspects "had the invalid been presentable [...] his father would have permitted him to come" to Thrushcross Grange, but Heathcliff hides Linton's poor heath as it may impede his marriage prospects. Heathcliff treats Linton "tyrannically and wickedly," again contrasting Edgar in their role as fathers.

Chapter XXVI

On Nelly and Cathy's first sanctioned expedition to meet Linton, Edgar decides that they will meet at the signpost that marks the midway point between Wuthering Heights and Thrushcross Grange. Yet when Nelly and Cathy arrive, a herd-boy is waiting to inform them that Linton is only "a bit further." When they reach him, they are very close to Wuthering Heights and he looks far too feeble to be outside at all. He claims he is feeling "better" despite "panting" and "trembling." He is unable to hold any sort of conversation with Cathy. Disappointed, she asserts that she will leave, but he anxiously asks her to remain a little longer, telling her that she must relay his 'good health' to Edgar. He also asks her not to reveal his lethargy to Heathcliff as he is afraid of his father's anger.

Linton falls asleep and they wait for him to wake up before they can go home. She is upset that meeting her is like a chore for him because she thought he would be equally as excited as her. Suddenly Linton sits up, certain that he heard his father's voice. He reminds them to come next Thursday and continues to insist he is in better health than before. When Nelly and Cathy reach home, they decide to keep Linton's health a secret until they can gather more information during their next visit.

Analysis

Linton's fear of Heathcliff is implied throughout the chapter, both through his constant but false affirmations of good health and his skittish behaviour. Coupled with Linton's "strange state of agitation" and insistence that Cathy stay, it is suggested Heathcliff has threatened the boy and is using Linton to accomplish his own goals.

Chapter XXVII

A week passes and Edgar's death is almost certain. Cathy spends all her time with him, realising her father will soon pass. Convinced that meeting Linton is a happy event for his daughter, Edgar allows her to go back to see him. Internally, he feels relieved that she will not be alone once he is gone. Nelly knows that he thinks highly of Linton because of the letters the boy sends him, but again speculates that Linton is incapable of writing so eloquently. Still, she keeps this information to herself, allowing her master to view Linton as a commendable nephew and potential husband for his daughter.

Cathy is determined to make her visit short and when she sees Linton he immediately brings up their lateness and Edgar's illness. She is angry and resolves to leave, since he clearly does not want to see her. He begins crying and begging her not to leave; it is clear he is hiding something. She asks him to be clear, naïvely certain that he would not endanger her safety. Then, Heathcliff descends upon them.

He asks how long Edgar will live, revealing that he worries Linton will pass before him. He instructs his petrified son to stand and for Cathy to kindly walk him to the house, but she refuses. He then asks Nelly, but she does not want to abandon her charge. Linton begs his cousin, saying "I'm *not* to re-enter [the house] without you!" and finally she agrees, walking him into the house and helping him to a chair. Nelly waits at the threshold ready to leave but Heathcliff pushes her inside and locks the door.

He tells the guests that Joseph, Zillah, and Hareton are out, and he wants company. Cathy tries to snatch the key from him, but he stops her and slaps her head multiple times, threatening that as he "shall be [her] father" in a few days. Nelly tries to interfere, but Heathcliff pushes her away, so Cathy seeks solace in her embrace. Suddenly calm, he tells Nelly to pour some tea for them all while he fetches their horses.

When he leaves, Nelly and Cathy try to escape but find all the doors bolted shut and the windows too small. They implore Linton for an explanation, but he refuses to say anything until they serve him tea. He is no longer afraid as he has clearly fulfilled whatever duty Heathcliff prescribed him. Linton tells them that Heathcliff plans to have them married the next morning and that they must stay the night. Nelly is furious and shakes him, inducing a coughing fit and some scolding from Cathy. Cathy resolves to burn the door down if she has to. Before any action can be taken though, Heathcliff returns informing them that their horses have disappeared.

Letting Linton go to his room, Heathcliff turns to his visitors (or more accurately prisoners). He delights in keeping Cathy from Edgar, who is awaiting her return and will be worried. He refuses to let her go until she is married. He also laughs at the letters Edgar wrote to Linton and his request that Linton be "kind to [Cathy] when he got her." The truth, Heathcliff reveals, is that "Linton requires his whole stock of care and kindness for himself" and can act a "little tyrant."

Cathy kneels in front of Heathcliff and acquiesces to the marriage so that she can see her father before he dies. While she begs there is a sound from the gate and Heathcliff rushes out to see what is happening. When he comes back, he cruelly tells them that the visitors were from Thrushcross Grange and they had missed their chance of escape. The two of them are told to stay in Zillah's chamber until morning, but neither can sleep.

The next morning, Heathcliff takes Cathy away but Nelly remains locked up. Hareton brings her food, but he does not help Nelly despite her pleas. She remains locked up for five nights and four days with no news of what has happened outside of her chamber.

Analysis

This chapter highlights Linton's selfishness and Cathy's love and devotion to her father. Linton's participation in Cathy's capture is stark evidence that he fears his father's wrath. We also get confirmation that the contents of Linton's letters were (at least in part) false, as Heathcliff no longer needs to hide Linton's true nature – he is neither as kind or gentle as his letters suggest, but instead cunning despite his helpless exterior. Although he really is sick, he plays up his illness and fear.

Cathy falls for his pretence when he sinks "prostrate again in another **par-oxysm** of helpless fear" and begs her to escort him to the house, but upon achieving his goal regains his composure. He also does not seem to care when Cathy is physically punished. Her kindness is not valued by Linton and is only used for his own benefit; we see this a little later too once they are married.

Chapter XXVIII

On the fifth afternoon, Zillah finds Nelly and tells her that everyone in the village believes she was lost in a marsh and that it is lucky Heathcliff found her. This is part of Heathcliff's plan – he has allowed Zillah to free Nelly so she can deliver a message to Thrushcross Grange informing Edgar that his daughter will be able to attend his funeral. Nelly is overjoyed to know Edgar is still alive, and she runs down to find Cathy and go home. Downstairs, Linton explains that he will not let Cathy go because she is now his wife, no matter how much she cries "she shan't go home!" Nelly tries to remind him of Cathy's kindness, hoping he will show her kindness in turn, but refuses to help her as her crying annoys him. Nelly determines him a "heartless, selfish boy," a "wretched creature [who] had no power to sympathise" with Cathy.

He gloats about how everything Cathy thought she owned will soon be his. He even attempted to take her locket, containing a picture of her mother and father, from her neck. Unable to obtain the key, Nelly hurries home, resolving to bring help from the Grange to rescue Cathy.

At home, Edgar is the "image of sadness and resignation" longing to see his daughter one more time before he dies. Nelly informs him that she should be home that night. She briefly tells him of their captivity at Wuthering Heights, purposefully leaving out Heathcliff's brutality and Linton's selfishness to avoid causing him further unnecessary pain. Edgar, still unaware of Linton's ill health, cannot see why Heathcliff rushed the marriage but knows his ultimate plan is to secure all of Cathy's wealth as his own. To prevent this, he decides to alter his will stipulating that her inheritance will be placed in the hands of trustees, thereby making sure Heathcliff and Linton cannot touch it.

Nelly sends a man to the village to fetch Edgar's lawyer, but the man returns without him, claiming that the lawyer will visit the next morning. She also sends four men to Wuthering Heights to rescue Cathy but they return empty-handed, believing Heathcliff's fabrication of Cathy's illness.

Nelly resolves to "storm" the building the next day, but thankfully she does not have to. In the early hours of the morning, Cathy arrives at Thrushcross Grange, desperate to see her father. Nelly sits her down and instructs her to pretend to be happy with her new husband to save her father from further sadness. Once Cathy is in Edgar's room, Nelly gives them privacy. Soon after seeing his daughter, Edgar passes away peacefully, happy to be "going to her" (his wife Catherine). Cathy remains at his side until brought away.

The lawyer arrives and the household learns that he has "sold himself" and his allegiance to Heathcliff. He has been to Wuthering Heights to receive orders from Heathcliff and as a result instructs all servants except Nelly to quit. He also insists Edgar be buried in the chapel with the rest of his family, but luckily his will and Nelly's protests ensure he be buried beside his wife. Cathy explains to Nelly that "her anguish" convinced Linton to help her escape, and that he was likely suffering for coming to her aid.

Analysis

Linton's selfishness and cruelty is highlighted in this chapter as he boasts about everything he has gained from his new marriage. He takes pleasure in owning everything that once belonged to her, especially the items that hold great sentimental meaning to her, such as her pony, locket, and books. He is glad to see his father strike her as "she deserved punishing for pushing [him]." Furthermore, when she cries Linton cannot stand it. This is ironic as he often behaves in a worse manner than her, crying about almost everything. However, he cannot "bear it" seeing someone act in the same way.

A final significant moment of this chapter is Edgar's death, which is described as "entirely without a struggle." His profound connection with Cathy is depicted through his desire to stay alive until able to see her again, passing away shortly after. We see her mutual care for her father as she lies about her misery, telling him that she is satisfied with her marriage to prevent him from suffering during his final hours. **The kindness, respect, and love in this father-daughter relationship makes it one of the purest relationships in the text,** contrasting Linton and Heathcliff's abusive relationship.

Chapter XXIX

Following the funeral, Cathy and Nelly request Linton live with them at Thrushcross Grange, at least until the boy dies. Heathcliff walks into the house unannounced, entering "the same room into which he had been ushered, as a guest, eighteen years before," but this time as master of both estates. Cathy tries to run away but he stops her; he is here to take her "home." He tells her that Linton is her "concern now" because he wants nothing to do with the boy.

Nelly suggests the young couple stay at the Grange since Heathcliff abhors them both, but he refuses, explaining that he is looking to get a tenant for his newly acquired property. He also wants her to make herself useful at Wuthering Heights, especially after Linton inevitably dies. Cathy vows not to let his attempts to drive a wedge between her and Linton ruin her love for him, but he reminds her that Linton's bad behaviour will do that itself.

When Cathy packs her belongings, Nelly begs her new master to let her and Zillah swap places so that she can stay with them at Wuthering Heights. He ignores her plea and focuses on the late Catherine's portrait hanging above the fire. He confesses that he went to her gravesite, which was uncovered during the digging of Edgar's neighbouring grave. He had opened her coffin and studied her unchanged face. Then removes the side of her coffin furthest from Edgar, so that he may be buried next to her in his own coffin (also missing its adjacent side) to be as close to her as possible. This experience revives his memory of the night after Catherine's burial, when he uncovered her grave to see her again.

He tells Nelly that he is certain ghosts exist because he felt Catherine's ghost beside him, bringing him immense comfort. Since that day, he has been tormented by her ghost thousands of times, no matter where he is or what he is doing. He takes the portrait down and instructs it delivered to Wuthering Heights. As Cathy returns, ready to ride her pony, he tells her that there will be no need for her pony at her new home and her "own feet will serve [her]" implying she won't be going far. Cathy asks Nelly to visit her when she can, but Heathcliff opposes this and quickly drags her away.

Analysis

In this chapter, Brontë explores the beginning of Heathcliff's decline as he reveals his experience with Catherine's 'ghost'. At this point it is up to the reader to speculate whether this should be interpreted as a real ghost or a figment of Heathcliff's imagination. The former insinuates that he and Catherine shared such a great bond while she was alive that even death cannot part them. The line between life and death is an interesting part of Gothic literature.

Conversely, if these 'ghosts' are simply part of Heathcliff's mind, it **symbolises his descent into madness.** He claims to have heard the ghost breathing, and can feel it everywhere he goes, causing him to lose sleep and proper functioning as he chases after it. All of these can be interpreted as signs that he is losing his grip on reality.

Chapter XXX

Nelly tells Lockwood that she has attempted to visit Cathy but was denied entry into Wuthering Heights by Joseph. The only information she can garner is provided by Zillah who does not like Cathy and her "haughty" manner. Nelly recounts her discussion with Zillah about Cathy's arrival at Wuthering Heights.

As soon as Cathy was brought to the house, she rushed into Linton's room without greeting anyone and locked herself inside until morning. She came down to ask Heathcliff to send for the doctor the next morning, but he refuses as "[Linton's] life is not worth a **farthing.**" Heathcliff tells her to either nurse Linton or abandon him, but never to speak about him again. She also asks Zillah for help. Despite pitying her, Zillah dared not interfere at risk of losing her job.

Farthing: a small, outdated coin worth a quarter of a penny. In AUD, a farthing is worth less than a fraction of a cent.

One night Cathy woke her up with instructions to tell Heathcliff his son is near death, but in her fear Zillah does not act until 15 minutes later when the bell in Linton's room rings. Having disturbed Heathcliff, he and Zillah discover Linton dead, with Cathy beside him. She was bitter due to her "struggle against death alone" and stays in her room for two weeks after Linton's body is taken away. Heathcliff comes only once to show her Linton's will, which bequeaths all his assets to his father.

Nelly speculates that he was coerced into this while Cathy was away for Edgar's funeral. The only asset he could not claim was his land (as he was still a minor) so Heathcliff claimed it under Linton's wife's name, leaving Cathy **destitute.**

Destitute: having nothing; extremely poor.

The girl finally came downstairs on a Sunday when Heathcliff left to visit Thrushcross Grange, and Zillah decided to stay home from church to be with her and Hareton. The young man immediately tried to make himself as presentable as possible for his cousin, cleaning up his dirty clothes and surroundings. Both he and Zillah offered Cathy their seats when she came downstairs, but she ignored them and brought herself another chair. She tried to choose some books from a shelf, but they were too high for her to reach. Hareton helped her, and stood behind her, studying the book she was reading, eventually focusing his attention on her hair.

He reached out to touch her curls and she got angry at him and sent him back to his seat. After a while, Hareton asked Zillah if she could request Cathy read to them – without mentioning his name. Zillah asked but made sure to express that it was Hareton's desire, not hers. Cathy rebuked their attempts at kindness and civility thinking them a "pretence," and has since become hated by all who live at Wuthering Heights. "The more hurt she gets, the more venomous she grows."

Nelly tells Lockwood that she wants to buy a cottage so that Cathy may come live with her. However, she knows that Heathcliff will not permit this, so the only way for Cathy to be free will be for her to marry again.

As Nelly's story concludes, Lockwood decides he will ride to Wuthering Heights as soon as he has recovered to inform Heathcliff that he will be going to London for six months. He does not want to spend another winter in this environment and would like to advise his landlord to find another tenant once his lease is complete.

Analysis

This chapter sees the same sullen and brusque Cathy that Lockwood met at the beginning of the novel, showing how her trauma from being surrounded by death and suffering has affected her. She is no longer as innocent or happy as when she first visited Wuthering Heights. She has lost her wealth and is now at the mercy of its inheritor – Heathcliff. She is orphaned and widowed, living in a household that hates her. Her refusal to accept Hareton and Zillah's peace offerings can be attributed to scepticism and distrust since they refused to help her when she *truly* needed it. She may also be wary of ulterior motives after Linton and Heathcliff trapped her and coerced her into marriage.

We have established **wealth is a major determinant of power, and Brontë exaggerates this** through Heathcliff's evaluation of his son as worthless (unable to amount to even a "farthing") and Cathy's powerlessness as she is 'moored' by Heathcliff's control.

Notably, there is a major change in Hareton's character in this chapter. He tries to make himself "agreeable" to Cathy and adopts a gentler manner. However, after she chides him, he quickly returns to his usual self, restoring his barriers to protect himself from further hurt.

Chapter XXXI

Lockwood visits Wuthering Heights again, carrying a note from Nelly to Cathy. Hareton opens the gate for him and accompanies him inside acting as a "watchdog, not as a substitute for the host." Cathy is preparing vegetables for their dinner and ignores his greetings. She sits by the window when she is done and Lockwood casually drops the note onto her lap. She flings it to the floor, unopened, and asks him what it is. Once he reveals it is a note from Nelly, Hareton grabs it and stores it away for Heathcliff to check. The girl pretends to cry, evoking her cousin's compassion. Hareton gives her the note and she happily reads it, directing a few questions to Lockwood.

He asks her to respond to Nelly, but she cannot because there are no reading or writing materials for her to use. Heathcliff does not read and as such "took it into his head to destroy [Cathy's] books." She tells him that she found a few books in Hareton's room. She berates him, likening him to a bird that "gathers silver spoons, for the mere love of stealing" because he cannot read. He is ashamed of this, and Lockwood tries to smooth the conflict by reminding her that Hareton is eager to learn. Cathy continues to mock him so he brings her the books wanting nothing to do with them. The girl refuses them, believing them tainted, and continues to anger him until he flings the books into the fire. Hareton is evidently upset at this "sacrifice" and his loss of "triumph and ever-increasing pleasure" of reading the now-burning books.

Hareton sulks away, briefly encountering Heathcliff. Heathcliff mumbles, oblivious to Lockwood's presence, that Hareton reminds him too much of Catherine. As Cathy sees him walking in, she leaves too.

Lockwood tells Heathcliff that he will pay his rent for Thrushcross Grange for the twelve months they had previously agreed upon but will not be returning. Heathcliff is fine with that and invites him to have dinner since "a guest that is safe from repeating his visit can generally be made welcome." He tells Cathy to get dinner ready and for her to dine with Joseph. Lockwood eats with Heathcliff and Hareton, eager to depart through the back door so that he can see Cathy one more time, but he does not get the chance.

As Lockwood rides away from Wuthering Heights, he muses about how wonderful it would have been for Cathy to fall in love with him so that she could escape her dreary lifestyle.

Analysis

Hareton and Cathy's relationship is full of angry clashes as both have reason to dislike the other. Cathy is upset with Hareton for standing by and allowing her to suffer under Linton and Heathcliff, and for 'stealing' her remaining books.

Meanwhile Hareton is humiliated by her constant jabs at his illiteracy and her mockery of his attempts to rectify it. This quickly turns violent, showing the **incendiary** nature of their relationship.

Incendiary: prone to starting a fire, or in this case conflict.

Cathy has gone from a sweet girl to a vicious and angry young lady. Her residence at the Heights seems to bring out the worst parts of her. **Brontë often uses her settings as a mirror for her characters** and Cathy adheres to this pattern, allowing herself to feed on the bitterness and animosity that pervades Wuthering Heights.

We also notice Lockwood's arrogance as he muses: "what a realisation of something more romantic than a fairy tale it would have been for Mrs. Linton Heathcliff, had she and I struck up an attachment." This reveals his inflated self-perception as Cathy's potential saviour and reminds us that his **self-interests bias the telling of story**.

Chapter XXXII

That September, Lockwood is passing through, close to Gimmerton, and decides to spend a night at Thrushcross Grange so that he can settle his affairs with Heathcliff. Arriving at the estate, he asks for Nelly, but the new housekeeper tells him she is now at Wuthering Heights. The frazzled lady sets about making him comfortable and cleaning a bedroom for him. He has many questions for her but she is too busy cleaning to answer any, so he decides to walk to Wuthering Heights.

Upon his arrival, he finds the place much more welcoming – the gate, door, and lattices are open and there are lovely smells coming from the fruit trees. He can see and hear two of the residents talking inside, one teaching the other to read the word "contrary." The young man (Hareton) learning to read is well-dressed and handsome, and the beautiful girl (Cathy) teaching him to read stands behind him. The couple are about to set off for a walk over the moors, and Lockwood does not wish to disturb their peace, so he goes around to the kitchen to seek entrance.

There he finds Nelly and Joseph, taking the former by surprise. She wishes he had informed them that he would be staying so that Thrushcross Grange could be ready for his arrival, but he does not mind. She explains that Heathcliff asked her to come to Wuthering Heights because Zillah left.

To Lockwood's surprise, Cathy is now in charge of affairs (and thus his rent), and Nelly is helping her learn how to manage. He learns that Heathcliff died three months ago. When Nelly came to Wuthering Heights, she "smuggled" over many books and other forms of entertainment from Thrushcross Grange to keep the girl happy. She also scolded Cathy's poor treatment of Hareton.

Heathcliff had become more withdrawn and spent most of his time away. An injury to Hareton's arm had left him confined to the kitchen, near the fireplace, and Cathy had found every excuse to be near him.

One day, she tried to tell him that she was happy to be his cousin and that she never meant to upset him, but he was still too angry at her to accept her advances. Nelly tried to convince him to be nice to her, but he again refused.

Cathy thought he hated her and he thought she hated him. He explained to her that he always took her side in any arguments against Heathcliff, and she apologised for her poor attitude. He still did not want to shake her hand so she kissed his cheek, leaving him flustered. She wrapped one of her books and addressed it to him, asking Nelly to deliver the present to her cousin with the offer that she would teach him to read. After some convincing, Hareton agreed, and the two became friends.

Despite a few hiccups (and to Joseph's disgruntlement), Cathy and Hareton's relationship blossomed to what it is today. Nelly is glad Lockwood did not try to win Cathy's heart, as during the cousins' union "[she] shall envy no one on their wedding day: there won't be a happier woman than [her]self in England!"

Analysis

Brontë signifies a new period of life at Wuthering Heights with drastic change in setting. Lockwood's walk to the estate is made enjoyable by the "splendid moon" and "a fragrance of stocks and wallflowers." The gate "yielded to [his] hand," providing little resistance to his intrusion, wherein previous chapters it was often locked – a physical and metaphorical obstacle isolating Wuthering Heights. This imagery implies its residents are happier, free from Heathcliff's terror; this contrasts with the initial description provided in chapter I, where the house was like a fortress.

The house has always reflected its residents, and previously, under Heathcliff's care, it was dark, closed off, and foreboding, indicative of his sullen and introspective nature. Now that it belongs to Cathy and Hareton, it is filled with love and openness, which is represented by the pleasant smells, pleasing flowers, and open doors and windows. As Nelly recounts to Lockwood how the young couple fell in love, she explains how their mending relationship gradually brought about this complete change.

Chapter XXXIII

Nelly continues her story by telling Lockwood that the very next morning, Cathy and Hareton dug up part of Joseph's garden to plant flowers from Thrushcross Grange. Hareton offered to take the blame for it. Nelly warned them to be careful in front of Heathcliff as he would punish them both.

All seemed well until Joseph walked in, fuming because Hareton destroyed his blackcurrant bushes. Cathy quickly jumped in and accepted responsibility for the mess but argued that Heathcliff could certainly spare her a fraction of the garden after he had taken all her land, and Hareton's too. She was sure that Hareton would defend her, but the boy tried to get her to leave before Heathcliff got violent. Still, she stayed, and Heathcliff grabbed her, telling Hareton to leave while he punished her. Hareton was torn between helping Cathy and obeying Heathcliff but before any action had to be taken Heathcliff let the girl go, demanding everyone stay out of his way.

Afterwards, Cathy tried to tell Hareton of how Heathcliff had usurped his land. However, Hareton begged Cathy not to speak ill of Heathcliff, as how would she like it if he same the same of her "father." She could see his loyalty to their oppressor was due to habit and conditioning, but decided to refrain from bad-mouthing Heathcliff in his presence.

From then on they became great friends and spent hours in each other's company, poring over books. When Heathcliff returned, they both looked up and the resemblance of their eyes to Catherine Earnshaw's shocked him so greatly that he sent them away peacefully. He asked Nelly to stay as he mused over his revenge on the children of his enemies. He explained to Nelly that despite acquiring both properties with plans to destroy them and the children's lives, he had "lost the faculty of enjoying their destruction."

He had also stopped caring about eating and drinking. All he had wanted for so long was to be one with Catherine, and as this desire had "devoured" his existence. Her face appears to be everywhere, not just in the resemblance of her living family members, but "in every cloud, in every tree – filling the air at night, and caught by glimpses in every object by day."

Despite his strength and physical health, he grew "only fonder of continued solitude" and Nelly surmised that guilt for his sins haunts him.

Analysis

Heathcliff's obsession with revenge seems to collapse as he has "lost the faculty of enjoying their destruction." This means he no longer enjoys causing the younger generation pain. Despite his relinquishment of the need for vengeance, **Brontë has long attributed Heathcliff's revenge as the catalyst of his downfall** and it is also during this period of his revelation that he begins to lose his sanity and desire to perform everyday tasks. He sees Catherine's ghost in "every cloud, in every tree" and cannot focus on anything other than her. This reveals how deeply his obsession has destroyed his life, as he no longer cares about living and dying and only wants to be with her again.

Nelly's guess that he may be experiencing guilt could also be true, as seeing Catherine's ghost can be **a symbol of his lack of closure** around her death and their relationship, as well as a constant reminder that he is hurting people close to her and potentially causing her pain. However, if he *does* feel any guilt, he does not overtly let on as he still holds resentment towards both children for their fathers' actions.

Chapter XXXIV

Heathcliff begins to eat less and less, and one night in April he left the house and did not come back until the next morning. Cathy and Hareton were out in the garden, tending to their flowers. The girl had run down to the gate to fetch some primrose roots and came running back to announce Heathcliff's return. She is shocked because he appeared "excited, and wild, and glad." Nelly went inside to see this sight for herself and tried to convince the man to have some breakfast. He claimed he was not hungry and did not want to be disturbed.

That night, he appears ready to have dinner with everyone, but quickly abandons his plateful of food to walk outside in the garden. Hareton went out to check on him, but Heathcliff sent him inside to be with Cathy. He re-entered two hours later still with the "unnatural [...] appearance of joy." He warned her to keep everyone away from him, and so spent the afternoon alone.

At 8 o'clock, Nelly goes to bring him supper but she is terrified by his "smile, and ghastly paleness," and sends Joseph instead. However, he returned with the (uneaten) dinner tray, instructing that Heathcliff be left alone. The master's footsteps could be heard going up to a specific bedroom with a window wide enough for him to climb out of and Nelly wonders "is he a ghoul or a vampire?"

Nelly then went to sleep and dreamt about Heathcliff's death and funeral, imagining his headstone simply read 'Heathcliff.' She adds to Lockwood that this came true as there was no information about his origins and age.

The next morning, Nelly realised he had not left the house, and thus brought him some coffee in the kitchen. He was still smiling and asked if they were alone. Upon hearing Nelly's affirmation, he pushes away the food and stares at something invisible, his gaze "anguished, yet raptured" following a moving apparition. Nelly insists he should eat and he tells her to leave.

Later, Nelly hears him talking to Catherine as though she was in front of him. She distracts him to draw his attention and he requests the lawyer come so he can draw up his will. Nelly again insists he eat and rest as he appears "starving with hunger and going blind with loss of sleep" and can leave his will for later. Heathcliff also wishes to be buried beside Catherine, even if they must do it secretly, with his burial attended by Nelly and Hareton but no minister.

Heathcliff soon becomes entirely antisocial and continued "groaning and murmuring to himself." So, Hareton fetches Dr Kenneth. The doctor comes and then goes as Heathcliff had locked his bedroom door, claiming that he was "better."

Two days later Nelly, out for a walk, notices Heathcliff's window open. It was raining so this meant he was likely out or otherwise drenched, so she goes inside to check. Opening the bedroom door, she found him "washed with rain [...] perfectly still" and smiling. One of his hands rested on the windowsill. She touched him and realised he was dead. No matter how hard she tried to close his "frightful, life-like" eyes, they would not shut.

Hareton sat by the body, crying all night, and Dr Kenneth could not pinpoint exactly what had caused Heathcliff's death. He was buried as he had wanted ("to the scandal of the whole neighbourhood"), and now his grave is covered with grass, blending into its surroundings. Many people have claimed to see his ghost out on the moors, including Joseph who is sure he sees Heathcliff and Catherine outside "every rainy night." Nelly herself is sceptical of ghosts, but she recently met a little boy on her way to Thrushcross Grange one night who was crying because he saw Heathcliff and a woman. Since this event, Nelly is eager to move back to the Grange with the soon-to-be-wed couple. She explains that Joseph will remain, with a boy to help him, at Wuthering Heights, but the main house will be locked up and they will stay in the kitchen.

Lockwood feels "irresistibly impelled" to leave without bothering the young couple as they return from their walk. On his way home, he makes a detour to the gravesite and sees the three stones marking the place of the bodies. The peaceful sight has him wondering how anyone could "imagine unquiet slumbers for the sleepers in that quiet earth."

Analysis

Heathcliff's change in behaviour from an angry and vengeful man to an excitable recluse comes as a shock. He seems liberated from his need for revenge and even his interest in his material surroundings. He can barely focus on thinking about his will, let alone the other (previously hated) residents of the house. He shuns Nelly's concerns for him to eat something and acts strangely such as walking outside all night and talking to an invisible someone (Catherine's ghost). Although we expect the household to be relieved at his new demeanour, everyone is unnerved.

The smile on Heathcliff's face after death adds to this effect. Joseph even refuses to touch the body as he believes "th' divil's harried off his soul" (the devil's taken his soul). **The stark and disturbing imagery Brontë uses here contradicts many of the other deaths that have occurred.** Both Edgar and Catherine passed away relatively peacefully, as though they were merely sleeping, but Heathcliff's description elicits revulsion and fear from the reader. All throughout the text he is depicted as strong and menacing, yet in his final days he seems to divert from this becoming "strange[ly] joyful." However, his true nature reveals itself once again upon his death.

The visitation of their ghosts suggests that Heathcliff and Catherine are once more reunited as they roam the moors together and sleep in the "quiet earth." Perhaps this is emblematic of their happiness, or perhaps they are trapped in purgatory together unable to truly attain "quiet" after death.

Section 4

Character Analysis

Heathcliff

Heathcliff is one of the central characters of the story. He participates in both arcs of the story across the two generations and is the reason for Nelly's recount to Lockwood. The text depicts his transformation from a silent orphan boy to the **abominable** man who ruins the lives of everyone around him. He is the Byronic hero of *Wuthering Heights,* characterised by his overpowering emotions, obsessive desires, and charming façade.

Abominable: detestable, loathsome, or terrible.

Let's focus on Brontë's development of his character and her effective creation of a famous Gothic hero.

We are first introduced to adult Heathcliff as a strange, cold, and rather animalistic man. Not only is animal (particularly dog) imagery used as a structural feature of the text, it is also frequently linked to Heathcliff. He growls during his first meeting with Lockwood and is later described as "wolfish" and in grief even gnashes his teeth and "foam[s] like a mad dog." Brontë frames him as wild, dangerous, and uncontrollable.

Race is an additional lens through which Heathcliff is viewed by other characters and Lockwood's initial impression of the character is quite conflicted as he is "a dark-skinned gipsy in aspect, in dress and manners a gentleman." As a child, he is ostracised by Old Mrs Earnshaw, Hindley, and Nelly for his skin colour upon his introduction to their household and later by the Linton family. Heathcliff is foundational in Brontë's discourse on race; she depicts him as a social outlier with the power to elevate his social standing (albeit through devious means). As an **expropriator** he leverages the Lintons' and Earnshaws' family wealth for his own means.

Expropriator: a person who takes away money or property, leaving nothing for the original owner.

Initially, he is a quiet child and "hardened [...] to ill-treatment," but uses his position as Old Mr Earnshaw's favourite to blackmail Hindley. Nelly initially thinks "him not vindictive" but in hindsight knows she "was deceived completely." Heathcliff's "genuine bad nature" is spotlighted throughout the text and he is truly "a most diabolical man, delighting to wrong and ruin those he hates." As a teenager, made servant by Hindley, Heathcliff is consumed by the need for revenge. Early on he shows a tendency towards violence and anger to express his dissatisfaction with his treatment. This morphs into the cruelty we see during adulthood. He takes advantage of Hindley's gambling addiction and usurps Wuthering Heights. His plan for revenge flows onto the next generation as he bars Hareton from an education, uses Linton as a puppet in his manipulation, and coerces Cathy into marriage.

However, we see some small glimpse of humanity in him as he pines for Catherine. He bursts into "an uncontrollable passion of tears" after Lockwood's encounter with Catherine's ghost, revealing genuine emotion aside from anger and displeasure. By portraying his character as wronged and angry yet grieving (and chasing after an **enigmatic** ghost) Brontë begins his characterisation as a Byronic hero.

Enigmatic: veiled in mystery.

Heathcliff loves Catherine deeply but feels threatened by the power dynamics of her superior status, especially when she befriends Edgar. It leaves him wishing for his "great blue eyes and even forehead." It is likely he desires the associated treatment and respect granted by this face rather than the appearance itself. Hearing Catherine reject him and accept Edgar's proposal only solidifies his envy because he believes he will never have Edgar's wealth and has now lost his love too. His rash decision to run away without confronting Catherine shows his heightened emotions and the extent of the isolation he feels. It hurts him to know that his financial and social status was the only hinderance in his relationship with Catherine, and thus works hard to amass a fortune before returning. He "struggled only for [her]," despite her engagement, and spent years growing his desire for vengeance. Obsessive tendencies and a fixation on self-destructive quests such as revenge are major characteristics of the Byronic hero archetype.

Another key aspect of the archetype is the otherworldly attractiveness which draws the affection of various women. Despite his physical beauty, the hero is still morally **reproachable** and a selfish lover. In Wuthering Heights, Isabella falls for this charm even though Heathcliff makes it abundantly clear that he is here to hurt her and her family. Without heeding the warnings of Catherine, Edgar, or Nelly, Isabella believes that the slightest affection Heathcliff bestows upon her is a sign he loves her. She marries him even though he is clear that he does not return her love, and he proceeds to abuse her for his "gratification."

Reproachable: something deserving of disapproval; cannot be justified.

He relents in the execution of revenge when he visits Catherine before her death. They argue, comfort each, and Heathcliff takes satisfaction in the knowledge that death will not part them. His crying and kisses are tender, which contradicts his usual demeanour. Romantic heroes in general tend to show a lot of emotion and experience everything very deeply, hence the impending loss of his love wounds Heathcliff to the core. She is his "soul," and he begs her to "drive [him] mad! only *do* not leave." This portends the lead up to his own death, where he envisions her still with him.

In the years following Catherine's death, Heathcliff does not present himself as a particular nuisance until Linton's arrival. Once Heathcliff has custody of his son, he uses physical intimidation to force the boy to obey him and court Cathy.

Initially Heathcliff seems to underestimate the bond between Cathy and Edgar, perhaps because he lacks true familial ties of his own. Thus, he takes matters into his own hands to force the girl into marriage. Nelly sometimes hopes that the memory of Catherine will stop Heathcliff from hurting her daughter, but he is so far gone by this point that he seems to see the girl as an extension of Edgar, rather than a person in her own right.

In the final chapters of the text, Heathcliff seemingly abandons the quest he has devoted his whole life to, having been driven mad by his need to see Catherine. He loses his viciousness and spends his time in an excitable and agitated state, seeing Catherine's ghost for days before his passing. While he claims to not feel any guilt for his transgressions, his eventual loss of sanity underscores that a lifetime of vengeance and obsession has brought about his downfall.

Catherine Earnshaw

Catherine is the only daughter of Old Mr and Mrs Earnshaw (the owners of Wuthering Heights). Her brother Hindley is seven years older than her. Her family 'adopts' Heathcliff when she is about six years old. As a child she is outspoken and mischievous, taking pleasure in running off into the moors with Heathcliff and avoiding stereotypical 'lady-like' activities. Catherine embodies the Romantic craving for freedom, passion, and oneness with nature – she wishes to be "a girl again, half savage and hardy, and free." Despite her death halfway through the novel, her influence pervades the lives of nearly every other character and can be viewed as equally destructive as Heathcliff.

In her life, she faces many complex decisions and situations, often at a young age, such as the death of her father, her feelings for Heathcliff, and her want for material satisfaction. She is often portrayed as vain and haughty but struggles to choose between what she wants most in life. As a result, she hurts those who care for her and unwittingly fuels a decades-long animosity.

Catherine first experiences conflict between her affection for Heathcliff and her budding friendship with the Lintons when she returns to Wuthering Heights after a five-week stay at Thrushcross Grange. After exposure to the privileged and luxurious life the Linton children lead, she begins to view her association with Heathcliff differently. This discrepancy is evident in the juxtaposition of her "very dignified person [...] displaying fingers wonderfully whitened with doing nothing" and Heathcliff's "dusky fingers" and dirtiness from "three months' service in mire and dust." Their appearance reflects their social status and the work (or lack of) they engage with. While Catherine evidently still cares for him, she spends more time with Edgar and Isabella, shunning her childhood friend. This shows that she greatly values social connections and material comforts promised by a future with the Lintons, however her fleeting thoughts towards Heathcliff remind her that she craves freedom and passion.

By the time she is 15 years old, Edgar proposes to her, forcing her to decide whether she values wealth, comfort, and 'seasonal' love over the "eternal" passion and fulfillment of Heathcliff's. She ultimately accepts the former's proposal. However, her motivations in doing so are to finance Heathcliff's escape from Wuthering Heights and she harbours no plans to be separated from him. Her indecision and desire to keep both men also exhibits her high self-esteem and certitude, sure that Heathcliff and Edgar will not question her decision.

Although she is torn between security and passion, she places more value on Edgar's wealth than Heathcliff's love believing it would "degrade [her] to marry Heathcliff." Yet, when he runs away she spends hours outside in the middle of a powerful storm, she searches for him and gets sick as a result. This underlines her connection to the natural landscape that surrounds Wuthering Heights, as the weather mimics her distress and exposes how deeply she cares for Heathcliff. The detriment of their parting is a recurring motif throughout the text shown through their grief, deterioration, the imagery of a shared soul, and ghostly hauntings.

She marries Edgar and the couple are presumably "in possession of deep and growing happiness," fuelled by Catherine's appreciation of her improved lifestyle and Edgar's desire to keep her satisfied. Nelly calls her a "thorn" among "honeysuckles" as she manipulates the entire household to bend to her will, indicating the incongruity between her **tempestuous** nature and the civility of Thrushcross Grange. When Heathcliff returns, she is overjoyed and completely sidelines her husband's concerns about her spending time with another man. Upon his arrival, she "flew up-stairs, breathless and wild; too excited to show gladness." While Catherine loves Heathcliff immensely, she is not blinded by her love. She easily points out his faults to Isabella, declaring him an "unreclaimed creature, without refinement." It is somewhat ambiguous whether she points this out to Isabella out of jealousy (to prevent their marriage) or as a genuine warning.

Tempestuous: characterised by turbulent emotion; related to stormy weather.

Catherine ends up losing her life due to her vanity and (partially) self-imposed destruction. Heathcliff and Edgar's anger appears to elicit a relapse of her dormant illness. As she succumbs to it, she revisits her childhood at Wuthering Heights, wanting to be outside on the moors where she felt happiest. Her connection to nature appears again when she says: "I'm sure I should be myself were I once among the heather on those hills." As a Gothic heroine, Catherine is naturally inclined to bond with the landscape around her; she recalls this tendency as she returns to her earliest self.

On her final night, she claims Heathcliff and Edgar have broken her heart; she is angry that she will die and Heathcliff will go on living the presumably happy and content life she had desired for herself. She states: "I wish I could hold you [...] till we were both dead! I shouldn't care what you suffered. [...] Why shouldn't you suffer? I do!"

This resentment and selfishness can be seen as the result of her lifelong desire to have both Heathcliff and Edgar – her icons of passion and security. Now disillusioned and heart-broken, she finds it hard to accept she has lost her chance to love either Edgar or Heathcliff fully.

After her death, Catherine manifests as a ghost, visiting Lockwood and Heathcliff on separate occasions. Her manifestation as a ghost on the moors is emblematic of her connection to nature, the weather, and landscape around her. It also alludes to her having fulfilled her dream "to escape into that glorious world" of nature. Yet, it is also demonstrating her connection to Heathcliff, as she fervently denies that death will be able to part them.

Catherine's constant battle between her need for material security and her desire for freedom may be a consequence of her position as a woman in the 18th century. Although she subverts gender roles in her childhood, being headstrong and free to roam the moors, and continues to do so more subtly as an adult by rebelling against the expected passiveness tied to womanhood and domestic arrangements, she still must marry to preserve and elevate her social status.

Edgar Linton

Edgar Linton is the only son and natural heir of magistrate Old Mr Linton and his wife. Isabella is his sister who is about three years younger than him. Edgar has grown up in a life of luxury and class, having been provided everything he could possibly want. His family lives at Thrushcross Grange, which is the finest house in the neighbourhood, decorated elegantly and maintained by a myriad of staff.

As a child, Edgar is sheltered and spoilt, completely ignorant of the feelings and problems of characters such as Heathcliff. We see this when he and Isabella start crying over who gets to play with their puppy, and through Edgar's undisguised comments about Heathcliff's appearance. Having grown up well-educated and taught proper manners, this may seem a little out of character; however, his dislike for Heathcliff may stem from the way everyone else around him responds. His parents dislike Heathcliff thereby instilling natural prejudice in him. Edgar and Heathcliff oppose each other in almost every way – social status, education, appearance, and temper.

Character foil: a character designed to oppose (and highlight) the traits of another.

Despite being a **character foil** to Heathcliff, the two are also intrinsically linked through Catherine. During Catherine's burial, Nelly intertwines locks of hair from (presumably) both men in her locket and returns it to the corpse. Edgar is laid to rest next to Catherine and Heathcliff on her opposite side. Brontë does, however, contrast the nature of their love for Catherine and their grief after her death. Unlike Heathcliff, Edgar does not reappear as a ghost despite the permeation of supernatural elements in the text. This could be interpreted in many ways – Edgar and Catherine's love cannot transcend death like her and Heathcliff's, or perhaps he is at peace in the "quiet earth."

As Edgar grows closer to Catherine in their teenage years, he seems to accept her for her tumultuous, and at times violent, personality and seems overjoyed when she agrees to marry him. He wilfully ignores her bad behaviour and develops "a deep-rooted fear of ruffling her humour," making sure no servants offend her over trivial matters that he himself does not care for. While Edgar avoids conflict with Catherine, she and Heathcliff argue throughout the text, even while on her deathbed.

In contrast, Edgar gives her "sympathising silence" in her "seasons of gloom" and reciprocates her joy with his own, showing he is greatly perceptive of her emotions. All these silent actions reveal how deeply he loves Catherine as he constantly places her comfort and happiness above his own. Brontë depicts Edgar's love as softer and healing, untarnished by obsession.

Edgar's parents pass away from the same illness Catherine caught after searching in the storm for Heathcliff. However, there is no indication that he resents her for this; instead, it is implied that he only devotes himself further to her in the three years Heathcliff is gone. When Heathcliff returns, he threatens the peace of Edgar and Catherine's marriage bringing with him countless memories of her love. Although "vexed" by Catherine's affection for Heathcliff, Edgar strives "to preserve his ordinary tone, and a due measure of politeness" because he is "gratified when anything occurs to please her." In some ways, it is honourable for him to respect Catherine's wishes but it is also an indication of his passive nature.

However, after Heathcliff disrespects his hospitality, Edgar asks him to leave. During this scene, Edgar experiences betrayal when Catherine insists he either fight or apologise. Both his wife and rival emasculate him by pointing out his slender form and his disinclination to violence. In an out-of-character display of violence, Edgar punches Heathcliff and leaves. While Brontë disrupts the meekness of the lamb imagery, she doesn't necessarily counteract the prey-predator positioning of Edgar and Heathcliff, but rather depicts Edgar's aggression as that of a cornered animal. We see how significantly Heathcliff and Catherine's relationship affects him; even "the most virtuous" can be "contaminate[d]" by Heathcliff.

Despite his fear of Heathcliff and his sons inheriting Thrushcross Grange, Edgar does his best to protect Catherine and Isabella (and later Cathy) from him, and it deeply injures him to know he cannot keep them safe. When Catherine falls ill, he is angry at Nelly for withholding this information and threatens to dismiss her. He also immediately forsakes his disappointment in his wife (stemming from their previous fight about Heathcliff) to care for her. Catherine says many hurtful things to him, including that he is "one of those things that are ever found when least wanted" and she is "past wanting [him]," yet he cares for her as best as he can. We have seen evidence of Edgar's ability to deal with heavy stress in a calm and collected manner in the interest of those he cares for. This is a commendation to his selfless nature and his unconditional love for his family.

Edgar is a devoted father. He gives Cathy a blissful but reclusive childhood, protected from all the dangers of the outside world. Up until his last moments, Edgar is focused on ensuring his daughter's safety and comfort after his death. Although he cannot amend his will in time, he takes solace in knowing his daughter is in a 'happy' marriage, despite knowing Heathcliff will usurp his property. He is happy to be with Catherine again and slips away peacefully, another stark contrast to Heathcliff's emotionally charged and "frightful" death.

Isabella Linton

Isabella Linton is Edgar's younger sister and the heir to his fortune (since he has no sons). She makes the tragic mistake of falling in love with a man who does not care for her. She has a "keen wit, keen feelings, and a keen temper, too, if irritated." While not as headstrong as Catherine, Isabella also subverts the patriarchal ideas that dominated society during Brontë's time of writing by escaping Wuthering Heights.

At the beginning of her marriage, she hates her life at Wuthering Heights so much that she wishes Heathcliff would kill her to end her misery; however, this transitions into a desire to kill *him* instead to free herself. Not only does she enter an abusive marriage where she does not have the power of the modern-day woman or grounds to file for divorce, she also marries lower on the social ladder to "a nameless man" (both literally in lack of surname and in status). This sees a further surrender of power to her new husband from her social mobility.

When presented with this opportunity to let Hindley kill Heathcliff, she passes it up, sticking to her moral code. She does not believe murder in cold blood could ever be forgiven, and hence does not help Hindley kill Heathcliff. Instead, she takes the fight as a chance to escape and build a new life for herself on the other side of the country. She gives birth to her only son, Linton, and cares for the sick child until she passes away of an unknown illness 12 years later.

In the 18th century, wives and children were seen as 'property' under their husband's guardianship and it was rare for a married couple to live separately. Physical domestic violence was normalised and as such Brontë shares insight into the female experience through Isabella's pain and suffering.

Isabella's impulsivity and stubbornness lead her to sacrifice her comfortable, pampered life at Thrushcross Grange for a tumultuous marriage with Heathcliff. She suffers the loss of her relationship with Edgar, which is never fully restored and does not get to see Cathy grow up. Although she is glad to be away from her suffering at Wuthering Heights, it is likely she also experiences great loneliness being away from her loved ones.

Hindley Earnshaw

Hindley Earnshaw is the oldest son of Old Mr Earnshaw, and Catherine's older brother. He inherits Wuthering Heights after his father's death, immediately taking action to demote Heathcliff to the social status of a servant. Despite this animosity towards his adopted brother, he is a caring husband to his wife Frances and looks forward to being a father.

When Frances dies, Hindley spirals into alcoholism and gambling addiction, feeding the danger and misery of Wuthering Heights. Brontë gives many kinds of grief a platform in *Wuthering Heights;* Hindley's is destructive as he copes through compulsive behaviours. He almost drops his infant son Hareton from the first floor and takes pleasure in beating or whipping Heathcliff. These actions incite the fire of vengeance inside Heathcliff and fuel the plot of the story.

Due to his gambling addiction, he mortgages his property to Heathcliff, leaving Heathcliff to claim ownership later in the novel. He is angry that Hareton does not have an inheritance and wants to kill Heathcliff for this but does not get to do so. To his dying day he is worried for his son's future but is tragically unable to do anything for him.

Hareton Earnshaw

Hareton is the last remaining Earnshaw, son of Hindley and Frances. He is uneducated and illiterate due to Heathcliff's manipulation. He works at Wuthering Heights doing the jobs Heathcliff delegates to him. Under Heathcliff's morally-skewed guardianship from a young age, Hareton seems to view him as a father-like figure – not an oppressor but rather a liberator. Heathcliff spends years conditioning Hareton to respect him, debasing him in a similar fashion to the treatment he also received as a child. He cuts off the boy's education, dispossesses him of his wealth, and positions him as a servant. Through the reversal of status, Brontë heavily embeds their relationship with irony. Despite a stunted social and academic education, Hareton exhibits a "generous heart" and "a mind owning better qualities than his father ever possessed."

Hareton is strong and capable of great intelligence and Heathcliff calls him "gold put to the use of paving-stones" and wishes he were his son instead of Linton. This strange relationship conflicts with Heathcliff's malice towards the boy's father and furthers Brontë's disassembly of Heathcliff's revenge. After his death Hareton grieves Heathcliff, "weeping in bitter earnest."

Unlike Heathcliff, Hareton seems mostly averse to exacting revenge. As such, Brontë enshrines his forgiveness and efforts of self-improvement as a conduit for redemption. While Hareton initially dislikes Cathy and Linton, his fascination with the girl eventually wins over as he tries to impress her by teaching himself to read. After Linton's death and Lockwood's departure, Cathy warms to him and takes over his teaching. This gentle offer sparks a friendship and eventually romance, granting both a rare happy ending.

Ellen 'Nelly' Dean

Nelly has been a servant at Wuthering Heights and Thrushcross Grange her whole life like her mother who was in charge Hindley's care. By the age of 13, she was already looking after Catherine and Heathcliff, and occasionally even Hindley. As she has witnessed the events that made Heathcliff who he is, she narrates her story to Lockwood, presenting herself mostly as a passive observer. Whilst on the surface this may appear true, a deeper reading of the text shows that Nelly's actions and inactions have a massive influence in the shaping the tale. By presenting herself as an observer, she may be trying to alleviate herself of any association or guilt for these events of the past.

The first major event occurring as a direct result of Nelly's choices is Heathcliff running away. While Catherine is giving her explanation for why she cannot marry Heathcliff, Nelly obscures his presence. Rather than clearing up the confusion and hurt feelings as quickly as possible to prevent further problems, she tries to hide this information from Catherine for as long as she can. The effects of this choice are drastic, and while it is not completely her fault that Heathcliff left, she may have prevented it. Occasionally, she incites trouble by withholding or sharing specific information.

Her disapproval of Catherine's behaviour often causes her to relay a prejudice account of events, inserting her own opinions, such as in Chapter XI when Heathcliff and Catherine are fighting. Similarly, in the days after the fight, Catherine stops eating regularly and insists that she is ill (she is also heavily pregnant at this time). Nelly seems to have reasonable cause to believe she is lying and delays relaying her condition to Edgar.

Despite her injection of bias into the story, she is a major character and acts as a surrogate mother to many of the children (particularly Cathy), seeming to care deeply for them. Although her dynamic as part of the family is interesting, due to her position as a servant she may be justifying her actions to protect her employment. As a joint narrator with Lockwood, their portrayal and perception of the text's cast is at times complex and discordant. Nelly's willingness to bend the truth to save herself likely impacts Lockwood's interpretation and subsequent narration.

Joseph

Joseph is the groundsman at Wuthering Heights, in charge of managing the gardens, farms, and general labour on the property. He has served the Earnshaw family for 60 years and takes a liking to Hareton. It is rare for Joseph to care for any of the children, as his main interest is the Bible and religion.

Joseph's religious inclination presents itself in almost every interaction he has, particularly through his speech which is populated by constant biblical references, prayers, and condemnations. It is interesting to see him seek solace in religion for natural occurrences such as storms and other weather **Pharisee:** a phenomena. He is also paranoid about the devil and witchcraft, making him hypocritical a naturally suspicious character. Joseph embodies the dwindling centrality person; alludes of religion in 18th century life which started to give way to the scientific to people who rationale of the Enlightenment. Through his generally disliked countenance strictly adhere as a most "wearisomest self-righteous **Pharisee**," Brontë explores and subtly to religious challenges strict, conformist views. observance without taking on the moral message of their beliefs.

Lockwood

Lockwood is a gentleman and tenant renting Thrushcross Grange from 1801 to 1802 from Heathcliff. He considers himself to be a quiet and socially awkward person, hence his desire to stay somewhere far away from urban life. He does indeed create awkward situations for himself at times, making assumptions about the relationships between Heathcliff, Cathy, and Hareton. Despite this, he seems inclined to make conversation and get to know those around him.

Lockwood's paradoxical behaviour starts with his desire to remain isolated from the world and his inclination to visit Heathcliff. He begins the novel by expressing his joy about being far from civilisation, labelling the moors a "perfect misanthropist's heaven," and describing Heathcliff as being "a man who seemed more exaggeratedly reserved than [him]self." This establishes his self-imposed identity as an outcast. The conflict arises when he begins to interact with other characters, as this reveals his tendency towards using formalities and a level of **garrulity** that one not would expect from an introverted and more socially-inept individual. Upon greeting Heathcliff, he immediately jumps into a verbose sentence introducing himself and his business at Wuthering Heights. Furthermore, on his second visit, he attempts conversation with Cathy politely and skilfully, demonstrating his *lack* of social awkwardness.

Garrulity: talkative; overarticulate when expressing simple ideas.

The quote: "I was encouraged so far as to volunteer another visit to-morrow. [Heathcliff] evidently wished no repetition of my intrusion. I shall go, notwithstanding," shows that he enjoys being with others, even when he knows his companions find him disagreeable. This particular action is laced with arrogance and strains his relationships.

His reliability as narrator is further brought into question by his narrow-mindedness. He tends to establish his perception of others based on superficial qualities, such as when he describes Heathcliff as "a dark-skinned gipsy in aspect, in dress and manners a gentleman" despite knowing nothing of his true character. He also takes an almost immediate physical liking towards Cathy, describing her as having an "admirable form, and the most exquisite little face." When faced with Hareton, however, he makes the "conceited" observation that the boy is "repulsive" in comparison to his own "tolerably attractive" nature. Although none of these thoughts are spoken aloud, we are presented with a clear picture of Lockwood's inflated sense of self through Bronte's characterisation of his prejudiced inner monologue. As the novel progresses, we hear little directly from him, however the snippets we receive show us that his nature does not change significantly.

Only at the very end in 1802 does Lockwood seem to accept Hareton and view him with respect and dignity. This may be due to the boy's newfound wealth and learning, or perhaps may be attributed to Lockwood's character growth. He laments passing up his chance "of doing something besides staring at [Cathy's] smiting beauty," having lost her to Hareton. Yet he is also happy that both youths found solace and joy in one another, allowing them to move on from the mistakes of generations past.

Catherine 'Cathy' Linton

Cathy is the only child of Edgar Linton and Catherine Earnshaw, sheltered in blissful ignorance away from urban society for most of her life. She is a kind, adventurous, and an extremely compassionate person who strives to improve others' lives and to lighten their burdens.

This brightness and innocence of hers is tainted when she meets Heathcliff and falls victim to his plans, giving way to a sullen and resentful young lady who laments her past. However, by the end of the novel, she reverts to her old self once again and devotes her time, attention, and affection to her loved ones. Her compassionate nature and lack of companionship fosters her naïveté and allows her to fall into Heathcliff's trap and be taken advantage of by Linton.

As a child, she "had not once been beyond the range of the park by herself," her only opportunities for such excursions being occasional walks with Edgar in the moors surrounding their home. She had never been to Gimmerton and had never heard of Wuthering Heights, Heathcliff, or anything about her family's conflict with him. Consequently, she lacks companionship with anyone her own age until she meets Linton.

When Edgar leaves for London, Cathy's rebellious urges overpower her cautious upbringing, causing her to discover Wuthering Heights. This event exposed some of her nastiness, stemming from her spoilt upbringing. She treats Hareton like a servant, expecting he be "made to do as [she] ask[s]" and was outraged upon learning he is her cousin. She is adamant her cousin is a "gentleman's son." This reveals she is used to being served and papered by everyone, and values status and appearance in her companionship.

Linton's arrival awakens mixed feelings due to his illness as he is too weak to play with her like she had planned. However, this disappointment disappears quickly as she infantilises her cousin by "stroking his curls, and kissing his cheek, and offering him tea in her saucer, like a baby."

During their relationship she plays nurse with Linton and is manipulated by Heathcliff's interference. Brontë weighs Cathy's romantic love for Linton with her familial love for her father. Cathy "care[s] for nothing in comparison with papa" and spends hours tending him prior to his death. This is a departure from her mother's characterisation whose romantic love trounced all her other relationships. However, like her mother, Cathy feels the need to take control of her own life and sneaks out to Wuthering Heights in the evenings.

While her compassion (imbued with naïveté) allows Heathcliff to lock her and Nelly in Wuthering Heights, Brontë does not position her kindness as a flaw. Instead, she further villainises the characters of Heathcliff and to an extent Linton (who can also be regarded as a victim) in their preying on her empathy and compassion.

After Edgar and Linton's deaths, Cathy changes dramatically from a self-sacrificial wife, nursing Linton, to a bitter and resentful widow who could "feel and see only death." However, like Hareton, she slowly moves past the tragedies and hardships in her life by seeking peace (instead of revenge) to process previous conflict. In doing so, Brontë shows how her good deeds (such as teaching Hareton to read) transform Wuthering Heights, welcoming back beauty, life, and love.

Linton Heathcliff

Linton is the only child of Heathcliff and Isabella Linton. He lives with his mother for most of his life until he is brought to Wuthering Heights to live with his father. From his birth, he's described as "an ailing, peevish creature" whose ill health remained with him until the tragic end of his short life. Although not much is known about his upbringing with Isabella, some inferences can be made from his behaviour. It is highly likely that his illness caused Isabella to spoil him and bend to his every whim, which forms his expectations of his new family. By the end of his life, Linton's selfishness and spoilt nature shine through as he uses these qualities to hurt others and secure self-preservation.

When he first arrives at Thrushcross Grange, Linton is sick and grieving. As Cathy started showing him affection, he "dried his eyes, and lightened into a faint smile," enjoying the attention. At this point it appeared to be an innocent reaction to his cousin's attempts to cheer him up, but as the story progresses it is clear he purposefully uses his condition to garner sympathy.

Despite his role in deceiving Cathy, he is sometimes successful in arousing pity in other characters and us as readers. He is often presented as a feeble creature who will "scarcely last till [. . .] eighteen" and implores Cathy to visit him telling her "to walk four miles would kill [him]." He also begs Nelly not to leave him at Wuthering Heights where his father, "bitterly disappointed with the whey-faced, whining wretch," abuses him.

Although he is a victim of Heathcliff's anger, Linton is soon rendered an imitation of his father's violence and misery. He jumps on the opportunity to demean Hareton, calling him a "colossal dunce" and he often acts "on purpose to distress his cousin." However, his "pettishness [. . .] yield[s] to a listless apathy" living a resentful and bitter existence, peppered with immense fear of Heathcliff. He begs Cathy to hide his declining health from Edgar for fear of invoking his father's wrath. The construction of such a façade preys on Cathy's compassion and serves as a significant survival tool for Linton.

His true selfish nature is irrefutable when he revels in Cathy's punishments and his possession of her belongings, "her pretty birds, and her pony Minny." He takes great pleasure in forcing her to break her locket containing her parents' portraits, and is disgusted by her sadness, illuminating his **avarice.**

Avarice: an insatiable greed for material objects and wealth.

From this broad overview of Linton's character, Brontë establishes him as a weak-willed, selfish, but admittedly cunning young man. Despite his short life, Linton plays a significant part in Cathy's journey and serves as a vital tool for Heathcliff's revenge. It is difficult to discern whether this cruelty was always inside him or if it simply developed out of necessity for his survival at Wuthering Heights.

Section 5

Key Themes Analysis

The sublime

The sublime is a complex philosophical concept, which can be simplified as an awe-inspiring and potentially terrifying force beyond human understanding. Usually, in Romantic and Gothic texts, the sublime is portrayed as a natural force that is stronger than humans. Some common examples are deep oceans, violent thunderstorms, and the view from the top of a cliff. Picture something that is immensely beautiful but equally dangerous.

Throughout Brontë's *Wuthering Heights,* the sublime is embodied in nature, in setting, and in characters' relationships. It is also well contrasted with the notion of civilisation and propriety.

The physical setting of *Wuthering Heights* is the most identifiable use of nature and the sublime to create a Gothic atmosphere. From the very first chapter, Brontë establishes the wild and uncontrollable weather that inspires the name of the novel and house. Wuthering is "descriptive of the atmospheric tumult to which its station is exposed in stormy weather," immediately introducing the powerful natural forces present in the area. We see Lockwood narrowly miss a snowstorm and Catherine's grief coincide with a rainstorm punctuated with "violent wind." As we have established throughout the Chapter Analysis, formidable weather events are often beholden to the characters' emotions.

The moors are also pivotal in Brontë's construct of the sublime. They act as a middle-ground between the Heights and the Grange, a wild interface between the civilisation of the two estates. The moors are a means of freedom and escape from social constructs such as race and class. While inherently dangerous, as even familiar travellers will "often miss their road," Catherine and Heathcliff (and later Hareton and Cathy) often wander the moors together. Putting this together, we can see the roots of this untamed landscape in forming the natural sublime.

The settings of Wuthering Heights and Thrushcross Grange are also contrasted in their furnishings, occupants, and meteorological incidence (read more on page 82). Thrushcross Grange is elegantly depicted and presents an image of civilisation and the epitome of upper-class luxury. The delicate furniture and refined residents are starkly different to the tumultuous personalities at Wuthering Heights. To complement this distinction, Brontë carefully presents the weather as mostly pleasant at Thrushcross Grange, except the blizzard and a few rainy days. Although this may seem trivial, Brontë interweaves **binary opposition** to contrast Thrushcross Grange (a beautiful property with good weather) and Wuthering Heights (a bleak property with volatile weather).

Binary opposition: a pair of mutually-exclusive things, often representing opposing ideas or values.

Catherine and Heathcliff's relationship is sublime in its immortality. Their passion is awe-inspiring, yet grotesquely marred by death, hatred, and destruction. Supernatural elements also endorse the other-worldly quality of their relationship as they return as ghosts.

Hence, nature and the sublime are important themes in *Wuthering Heights* and a hallmark of Gothic literature that often reflects the state of characters. By contrasting untameable forces with civilisation, Brontë uses the landscape to explore the different lifestyles and values within her characters.

Romantic love and obsession

Romantic love presents itself in many ways in *Wuthering Heights:* from Edgar's selfless devotion to Catherine, to Heathcliff's selfish but eternal love for Catherine, and Isabella's infatuation. Relationships such as Catherine and Heathcliff's or even Isabella and Heathcliff's can often err on the side of obsession for one or both parties, but it is important to distinguish between *love* and *obsession*. Love is generally understood to be an intense but positive feeling which fulfils a person and allows them to care unconditionally for another. A key aspect of love is the ability to maintain their individuality and autonomy (to an extent, considering this is 18th century England). Obsession, on the other hand, comes with heavily negative and unhealthy connotations as an all-consuming desire to possess an idealised form of love from another. Obsession often has more to do with power than love. Let's look closely at the main romantic relationships in the text.

Heathcliff and Catherine

Heathcliff and Catherine have an almost *sublime* bond, so strong that it transcends separation and death. Their relationship is filled with passionate dialogue, emotional suffering, and jealousy. During their childhood, after Catherine overcame her initial aversion to Heathcliff, they became the best of friends, seeking solace and comfort in one another during the hardships life threw at them.

As they grow up, there are various examples of their blossoming love throughout the first half of the novel. One of the most prominent examples of this is the "almanack" that Heathcliff hung on the wall in Chapter VIII, marked with crosses the evenings Catherine spends with the Lintons, and with dots the ones with him. Although this shows how deeply he values her attention, even though he makes a show of "recoiling with angry suspicion from her girlish caresses," it also reveals an obsessive desire to monopolise her time. In this same chapter, he actively refrains from insulting Catherine's "pitiful, silly friends" (any more than he already has), as he knows it will upset her. She shuns him, saying "it's no company at all, when people know nothing and say nothing," insinuating that he is too dumb for her. We might assume that rejection wounded Heathcliff's pride and further fuelled his obsession.

Despite acting dismissively, Catherine harbours immensely strong feelings towards Heathcliff, which she reveals to Nelly in her passionate speech in Chapter IX (on another note, see this chapter for some more great quotes on love!). Catherine states: "I love him: and that, not because he's handsome, Nelly, but because he's more myself than I am. Whatever our souls are made of, his and mine are the same."

She also describes this love as "necessary" and their separation as "impracticable." Their 'shared' souls may illustrate how they saw characteristics of each other in themselves as children.

It is at this point in the story that their relationship has fully morphed into obsession. Heathcliff runs away but is entirely motivated by two things: revenge and Catherine. He states: "I've fought through a bitter life since I last heard your voice; [...] I struggled only for you!" revealing the extent to which he has ruminated on her since their separation – he claims everything he has done has been for her. Once Heathcliff returns, their relationship begins to falter as his desire for revenge overrides their friendship. Catherine is angry when she finds out he kissed Isabella, paving a jealous pathway to Catherine's doom.

This obsession begins to destroy both parties as Catherine descends into illness, leaving Heathcliff grief-stricken. Despite her marriage, Heathcliff is possessive of even Catherine's thoughts: "for every thought she spends on Linton she spends a thousand on me." Furthermore, he adds that if Edgar "loved with all the powers of his puny being, he couldn't love as much in eighty years as I could in a day," revelling in the perceived superiority of his love.

While Brontë portrays their love as powerful, she cautions again their obsession by framing it as detrimental to Catherine's other relationships (particularly with Edgar) and coming at the cost of death. After her death, Heathcliff's pining for her continues for decades. In the garden, the morning after her death, he is already aware of her passing despite not hearing the news of it from anyone. This is a significant part of the transcendental and sublime bond between the two characters which, as Catherine mentioned earlier in the novel, is unhindered by separation or death. He begs for her to haunt him in an intense emotional display, where he cries:

QUOTES :
"Be with me always – take any form – drive me mad! only do not leave me in this abyss, where I cannot find you! Oh, God! it is unutterable! I cannot live without my life! I cannot live without my soul!"

This sentiment persists and he searches constantly for her presence: outside in the moors, at her gravesite, and even in her coffin. Through their relationship, Brontë elucidates the trauma generated by Heathcliff's childhood, and his search for superiority in all pursuits, even love. While their spiritual bond seems to reunite them in death, the all-consuming tone of their love hurts them both deeply in life, leading to the downfall of both characters.

Catherine and Edgar

The relationship between Catherine and Edgar was painful for both parties, despite their efforts to make it work. While Catherine may love Edgar, Brontë frames her affection as superficial, marrying him because he is "handsome, and pleasant to be with" and would give her the chance to become the "greatest woman of the neighbourhood." Meanwhile, Edgar genuinely loves and cares for Catherine, doing everything in his power to make her comfortable and happy. Prior to Heathcliff's return, Nelly believed "they were really in possession of deep and growing happiness."

Brontë presents Edgar as the opposite of Heathcliff. He appears a selfless lover who "lavished on [Catherine] the kindest caresses," placing his wife's needs before everything else, but the depth of his love is unrequited. Catherine takes advantage of Edgar's selflessness, manipulating his "deep-rooted fear of ruffling her humour." She feigns fits of illness and counts on his disinclination to anger or violence, allowing herself to continue her relationship with Heathcliff. This behaviour continues preceding her death, wanting to punish him for 'avoiding' her: "if I were only sure it would kill him [. . .] I'd kill myself directly!" Brontë characterises Edgar's love as noble but futile, as Catherine's affections are childish, vengeful, and short lived.

Cathy and Linton

Cathy and Linton have a stressful relationship plagued by their parents and Linton's poor health. Cathy's lack of friends her own age and good nature leads her to be very accommodating to Linton's various needs, even risking her own safety and happiness at times to make him happy. Aware of her compassionate nature, Linton uses her to care for him and as a **scapegoat** for Heathcliff's anger and abuse. We are led to believe Cathy prioritises the idea of having a well-educated and "pretty" cousin, which she uses as the basis for her love rather than forming a meaningful relationship with Linton.

Scapegoat: a person who is unfairly attributed the blame meant for others.

We may also suspect he holds an underlying jealousy towards her for her close relationship with her father, her peaceful upbringing, and her wealth, wanting all of these for himself. He is also disgusted to see her upset but expects her to care for his own feelings. This unbalanced relationship takes a toll on them, leading to Cathy's reclusive behaviour at the start of the text. The ill-fated pairing of the two is perhaps a comment on how external influences may negatively impact a relationship.

Cathy and Hareton

While this relationship doesn't start with love or obsession, by the end of the novel it grows into contented domesticity as Brontë grants at least one of her couples a happy ending. Where Cathy had previously mocked Hareton for being unable to read, in the final chapters she teaches him word by word and their "intimacy thus commenced grew rapidly." Their relationship seems to have a positive effect on both Cathy and Hareton; Cathy in her happiness, and Hareton in appearance, manner, and education – "his honest, warm, and intelligent nature shook off rapidly the clouds of ignorance and degradation in which it had been bred." The freedom they find in their connection with each other is mirrored in the freedom they find on their regular walks on the moors together.

Social class and race

Social class was a rigid but inherent aspect of life in Brontë's sociohistorical context, and hence plays a significant yet underlying part in most major conflicts. The rise of the Industrial Revolution challenged previously concrete class structures as it slowly encouraged the possibility of social mobility. Heathcliff's fortune is considered 'new money' and was largely frowned upon by the aristocracy and 'old money' families, such as the Lintons and to some extent the Earnshaws. Although set a century apart, think about the pervading social division between East Egg (Tom and Daisy Buchanan's old money) and West Egg (Jay Gatsby's new money) in *The Great Gatsby.*

People of colour, such as Romani people, migrants, and freed slaves were also discriminated against under this hierarchy. This blatant classism and racism inform the treatment Heathcliff receives from various characters such as Hindley, Catherine, and the Lintons. Upon his arrival at Wuthering Heights, Heathcliff is described as "dark almost as if it came from the devil" by his own adoptive father and Catherine spits on him. Luckily, he is brought up as one of the Earnshaw children and given access to an education. This changed when Hindley becomes master of the estate and degraded him to the status of a servant. Heathcliff's mistreatment during this time stays with him for life and is a driving factor in forcing Hareton into the same life of servitude. He gloats to Nelly by saying: "I've got him faster than his scoundrel of a father secured me, and lower; for he takes a pride in his brutishness."

This reversal of roles would have been extremely distressing in Brontë's context, as Heathcliff, a person of colour who grew up as a servant, is now inflicting the same fate on to his oppressor's higher class (and innocent) son. He almost successfully strips Hareton of his title, his education, and any chance of regaining his property by making the boy socially repugnant and an outdoor labourer. The importance of this change in social status is to show just how far Heathcliff goes in demeaning Hindley and his family.

Catherine also picks Edgar over Heathcliff as a result of social status, and her love of material wealth and luxury. She asks Nelly: "did it never strike you that if Heathcliff and I married, we should be beggars?" Brontë succinctly conveys how marriage dictates social status through Catherine's desire to be the "greatest woman of the neighbourhood." Her need to improve her social standing overpowers her love for Heathcliff.

Upon her return from her five-week stay at Thrushcross Grange, Catherine is changed into a "dignified person," influenced by the Lintons and her sister-in-law Frances. Her entire style of dressing changes to become more lady-like and refined, and she begins regular association with the Lintons. Her assumption of a new, more elegant appearance and demeanour marks her assimilation into the Lintons' rung of society.

From this brief examination of class and race, we can see the rigidity of the system brought pain, prejudice, and injustice. For most women, like Catherine, social class correlated with marriage prospects which could yield comfort and happiness through elevation of wealth and status. Generally, the more money you had the more respected you were, and you were able to live a better lifestyle.

During Brontë's time, it was common for women to attempt to find a husband who could provide them with everything they needed, and if they were lucky, one they liked. By finding and loving Edgar, Catherine made a reasonable decision to guarantee her and her children's future comfort, but in doing so she sacrificed her relationship with Heathcliff. However, Brontë still challenges the values of her time through Heathcliff and Catherine's ghostly reunion after death.

Vengeance and retribution

Vengeance is a key theme and motivator in the plot of *Wuthering Heights*. Being a Gothic text, Brontë devotes significant attention to the dark and destructive parts of human existence, presenting revenge as a conflicting ideal to love and a factor in the demise of various characters. Revenge is different from retribution as the former is motivated by anger or malice, while the latter by a need for justice.

Brontë presents Heathcliff as the most vengeful of all the characters as he concocts a long and difficult plan to destroy everyone who ruined his life. Catherine also has a **propensity** to manipulate others to get revenge on them for causing her discomfort. When placed together, their vices clash with their love for one another and ultimately lead to their destruction.

Propensity: an inclination towards something.

In Heathcliff's case, his obsessive need for revenge plays a significant role in his characterisation as a Byronic hero and Brontë delves into the impact of his archetypal destruction on the lives of other characters. Heathcliff's vengeance is his method of rising above Hindley and the Lintons to claim back the power and respect they denied him. He believes that it will bring him contentment and satisfaction to cause them to suffer as he did. However, his revenge leaves him 'blind' to joy – a reference to Isabella's desire to take an "eye for an eye, a tooth for a tooth" (despite not acting on this). Iterations of this phrase appear biblically (in Leviticus and Exodus), in pop culture, and has been famously spoken by politicians and the likes of Gandhi with the adage of risking blindness and toothlessness. At the **denouement** of the text, he has completely "lost the faculty of enjoying [...] destruction." This powerfully suggests revenge does not solve anything and only serves to further annihilate the perpetrator.

Denouement: the concluding or final part of a text.

Catherine's vengeful nature is pettier and more rooted in her vanity and need to be loved by both Heathcliff and Edgar. After her argument with them in Chapter XI, she decides to "break their hearts by breaking [her] own," deeming that they should suffer because they were angry at her. She locks herself in her room to elicit guilt from Edgar and wishes Heathcliff to suffer once she is gone. Even her ghost may be viewed as a symbol of revenge by the misery it causes Heathcliff. Accordingly, Brontë again pits revenge against love as the cause of demise.

Interestingly, Edgar does not seek revenge. He is in a position where his wife loves another man, one devoted to ruining his family and stealing his property. Yet he does not take unprovoked action to inflict misery on Heathcliff. In fact, he spends his life enjoying his time with his daughter and avoiding the presence of anything that would cause him to relive his pain. Edgar "had not the heart" to pass by Wuthering Heights, instead learning to move on from his grief. Brontë uses his noble aversion to revenge to contrast Heathcliff's obsession.

Hindley's revenge is also another, albeit more minor, thematic building block. He feels cheated out of his father's love and his property displaced in Heathcliff's hands. While he seeks revenge on Hareton's behalf, some readers may feel Hindley receives retribution for his bullying of Heathcliff and erratic parental behaviour.

Vengeance in *Wuthering Heights* is a complex theme used to facilitate destruction and Gothically encapsulates unhealthy obsession as harbouring darkness. Ultimately, though some other messages in the novel are more ambiguous, here Brontë presents vengeance as a clear path to devastation.

Supernatural

Supernatural forces are an important part of Gothic literature as they are often employed to speculate about the nature of death and the afterlife. Several characters refer to demons including devils, vampires, ghouls, goblins, and ghosts. Joseph, being a devoutly religious character, shuns the supernatural; he fears Cathy's threats of witchcraft and later refuses to touch Heathcliff's body believing the "divil's harried off his soul."

While trapped in Wuthering Heights, Nelly calls Linton a "pitiful changeling." In folklore, changelings were thought to be human-like substitutes left by faeries, pixies, or elves in the place of a stolen human child. This was a popular explanation for children born with disability or illness – it was easier for a family to believe their own child was happy and safe with the faeries, while the 'substitute' was dying. In Nelly's eyes, not only is Linton ill, but his deceptive and disturbing actions render him inhuman. She also questions Heathcliff's humanity as his mental health declines, musing about the undead and "hideous incarnate demons."

While we see the supernatural though the socio-cultural portrayal of the time, of course the most prominent supernatural feature in *Wuthering Heights* is Catherine's ghost. Brontë blurs the line between life and death as ghosts haunt the living, particularly to highlight the connection between Heathcliff and Catherine, and his decline as he approaches death.

Heathcliff and Catherine's bond is so deep that during the "most miserable period" of his life, Heathcliff was "haunted" with the knowledge that Catherine was thinking of him. It is so strong that the all-powerful forces of "God or Satan" cannot part them. Hence it comes as no surprise that physical barriers such as death or decay cannot hinder their supernatural, transcendental bond. Heathcliff does not "dread any change of that sort" and even looks forward to "dissolving with her" into the earth. He pleads for her to haunt him after she dies, which evidently, she does.

Brontë also uses supernatural elements to highlight Heathcliff's obsession with Catherine. From Lockwood's overnight stay at Wuthering Heights, wherein Heathcliff wept for her to come to him, to his final days, his ability to discern what is real and what is in his mind gradually diminishes. Nelly recalls his conversation with ghost Catherine as "spoken as one would speak to a person present," indicating that he truly thought Catherine was with him. Brontë elegantly leaves it open to the reader's interpretation whether there are really ghosts in her story, as the characters themselves are left questioning their beliefs.

The supernatural is used to enhance the Gothic and macabre nature of the novel, exploring the idea that death is far from an impenetrable barrier. Death is portrayed as a transient hiccup in the immortal love between Heathcliff and Catherine as she visits him and haunts him as a ghost. Sceptical interpretations of the text can view her 'ghostly' presence as hallucinations signifying Heathcliff's insanity as his obsession takes over his life. Yet, it remains that Brontë uses supernatural elements to add a spiritual and mystical sense to *Wuthering Heights*.

Structural Features Analysis

Nested narrative

Wuthering Heights has a unique and at times complex narrative structure that fluctuates between two main narrators: Lockwood and Nelly. The narration style can be described as *framed* or *nested*, which refers to having a story inside another story. Brontë does this by having Lockwood tell a story of his experience at Wuthering Heights with Heathcliff and the other characters and having him recount Nelly's story inside his own.

The effect of this technique is to shroud the characters being discussed in a veil of mystery and uncertainty. All the information we have is speculative and (potentially) very biased, having come from secondary sources (Lockwood and Nelly). Nelly reveals information according to her fancy; we do not learn of Catherine's pregnancy until she is already seven months. She also justifies her potential wrongdoings and frames them in a positive and excusable light.

Readers do not get to hear from any active participants in the tale, such as Heathcliff, Catherine, Edgar, or Cathy, about what truly happened firsthand, leaving us to discern between fact and fiction. This element of the unknown contributes to the Gothic ambiance of the story; nothing is certain, and it never will be as most characters are dead by the end.

Setting, imagery, and pathetic fallacy

Brontë uses vivid imagery and pathetic fallacy to create tangibly Gothic settings. These Gothic settings are characterised by darkness, isolation, and mystery. Her use of visual imagery presents a picture of a jagged, deformed, and unwelcoming landscape at Wuthering Heights, using words like "stunted" and "gaunt" to describe the surrounding plants. The furnishings of the house are "grotesque" and "villainous." This description of the **eponymous** house lends itself to personification which when combined with the exterior landscape, forms a foreboding and threatening atmosphere.

Eponymous: something or someone that a text is named after.

The use of pathetic fallacy and nature as a reflection of the characters' emotions also contributes to the Gothic setting, as Gothic characters often experience uncontrollable negative emotions. When Heathcliff runs away, a storm comes "rattling over the Heights in full fury," thereby using pathetic fallacy to reflect both his and Catherine's emotional distress as stormy "fury" in that moment. The "violent wind" and thunder bring an entire tree down on top of the house. This is a strong technique to physically manifest the characters' emotions.

Sackless:

innocent;

undeserving of

punishment.

Similarly, when young Cathy is distressed over her father's imminent death, Brontë reflects this in the gloomy, rainy weather, and the presence of a "melancholy" singular flower "as starved and **sackless**" as Cathy herself. This simile and visual imagery amplify the reader's understanding of her lonely and undeserved grief, again playing to the overarching aspects of isolation and suffering of the Gothic. Having weather and nature reflect human emotions – particularly the negative ones – is a structural feature Brontë uses throughout the novel to underscore the intensity of emotion felt by her characters.

Symbols and motifs

Wuthering Heights and Thrushcross Grange

Wuthering Heights is a dark, isolated building, situated on a hill in the moors far away from civilisation, symbolising the Gothic ideals of the novel. Its residents are equally as distant and peculiar, and the estate mimics its inhabitants. The building has "narrow windows," "grotesque" decorations, and "corners defended with jutting stones." It is surrounded by prickly flora such as "firs" and "thorns," reflecting the barbed nature of its residents (particularly Catherine who is also described as a "thorn"). Heathcliff, Catherine, and Hindley are all highly emotional and tumultuous people whose feelings are displayed in large, oftentimes violent and melodramatic fashion. When they reside at Wuthering Heights, the building becomes a symbol of darkness, isolation, and uncontrollable emotion seen through the "wild and stormy" nature of its people and landscape.

Conversely, Thrushcross Grange is beautiful, elegant, and well-maintained. "Thrushcross Park is the finest place in the world" with "soft, sweet air," and furnished with "crimson-covered chairs and tables, and a pure white ceiling bordered by gold, a shower of glass-drops hanging in silver chains from the centre." The imagery reflects the gentle and kind nature (and wealth!) of the Lintons in comparison to the residents of Wuthering Heights. The traditional beauty of the landscape and house is symbolic of the Linton's social class as gentry.

Brontë starkly distinguishes the two estates. We only begin to see change prior to Heathcliff's death when Cathy and Hareton start "planning together an importation of plants from the Grange" to create a new garden. Heathcliff's angry acceptance of this endeavour and his subsequent change in behaviour can be seen as a metaphorical transplant of values from Thrushcross Grange to Wuthering Heights. After his death, the Heights seem substantially transformed upon Lockwood's final visit, with a newfound openness that reflects the "pleasure" of Cathy and Hareton.

Ghosts

Ghosts represent a few concepts in the text, the most notable of which are the transcendental bond between Heathcliff and Catherine, and Heathcliff's descent into insanity. The former is portrayed by the presence of Catherine's ghost at various intervals, such as when Lockwood stays overnight and she seeks to come home, and at the very end of the novel when the little boy claims to have seen "Heathcliff and a woman" in the moors. Catherine's ghost constantly plagues Heathcliff and yet embodies the perseverance of their connection following her death.

Heathcliff's obsession with Catherine's presence after death is a motif that depicts his loss of sanity. He claims to have heard her "warm breath [. . .] displacing the sleet-laden wind" as he dug up her grave. Furthermore, in the days preceding his death, Nelly heard him speaking to her as though she was there with him. Each time Heathcliff mentions Catherine's ghost, he slips further and further into his obsession and insanity, thereby making it a symbol of his madness.

Some other interpretations include her ghost as a reminder of the guilt and pain Heathcliff has caused others, which now torments him in his final days. Coincidingly, Lockwood denounces her ghostly form as a "just punishment for her mortal transgressions" before knowing the full story. Her recurring presence could also represent the lack of closure and grief Heathcliff (and maybe Catherine herself) feel towards death and the loss of their imagined life together.

Graves and gravestones

Catherine is buried with Edgar and Heathcliff on either side of her by the end of the novel "on a green slope in a corner of the kirkyard." She is not buried in the Earnshaw tomb or with the Lintons in the chapel. The placement of her remains frames her as separate from both families, and away from civilisation, signifying her preference to be close to nature. Her proximity to the moors pervades both her life and death. Edgar is buried next to her instead of with his family. While a lasting testament to his love for Catherine, this can also be read as a rejection of his position in society; Edgar's grave is adorned by a "simple headstone" whereas the rest of the Linton family have a "carved monument" in the chapel – a recognition of their high class.

Heathcliff is also buried next to Catherine, which is to "the scandal of the whole neighbourhood" for an unrelated man to be buried next to a married couple. They are laid to rest side-by-side in a makeshift adjoining coffin, which Heathcliff achieved by bribing the sexton to remove the adjacent sides of their caskets upon his burial. As gruesome as this sounds, this again creates a contrast in Catherine's relationship with the two men. Edgar is still separated from Catherine by the in-situ walls of their coffins, much like he was in life by the superficiality of her love. For Heathcliff and Catherine there is no separation, and they remain right next to each other in death (as corpses and ghostly apparitions).

Another thing to note is the lack of a last name on Heathcliff's gravestone. Despite the fortune he amassed during his lifetime, he is still nameless in death. The only other information is the date of his death since his birthday is also unknown.

Section 7

Quote Bank

The sublime

Quote	Character	Chapter
"One may guess the power of the north wind blowing over the edge, by the excessive slant of a few stunted firs at the end of the house; and by a range of gaunt thorns all stretching their limbs one way"	Lockwood	I
"On that bleak hill top the earth was hard with a black frost, and the air made me shiver through every limb."	Lockwood	II
"Do you know that you run a risk of being lost in the marshes? People familiar with these moors often miss their road on such evenings"	Heathcliff	II
"Catherine marked the difference between her friends, as one came in and the other went out. The contrast resembled what you see in exchanging a bleak, hilly, coal country for a beautiful fertile valley"	Nelly	VIII
"Heedless of my expostulations and the growling thunder, and the great drops that began to plash around her, she remained, calling at intervals, and then listening, and then crying outright."	Nelly	IX
"The storm came rattling over the Heights in full fury. There was a violent wind, as well as thunder, and either one or the other split a tree off at the corner of the building"	Nelly	IX
"My soul will be on that hill-top before you lay hands on me again."	Catherine	XII
"The snow is quite gone [...] the sky is blue, and the larks are singing, and the becks and brooks are all brim full."	Edgar	XIII
"The abrupt descent of Penistone Crags particularly attracted her notice; especially when the setting sun shone on it and the topmost heights, and the whole extent of landscape besides lay in shadow."	Nelly	XVIII

~ SnapRevise® ~

"That was his most perfect idea of heaven's happiness: mine was rocking in a rustling green tree, [...] the moors seen at a distance, broken into cool dusky dells; [...] the whole world awake and wild with joy.	Cathy	XXIV
"The following evening was very wet: indeed, it poured down till day-dawn [...] I observed the master's window swinging open, and the rain driving straight in"	Nelly	XXXIV
"I sought, and soon discovered, the three headstones on the slope next the moor: on middle one grey, and half buried in the heath; Edgar Linton's only harmonized by the turf and moss creeping up its foot; Heathcliff's still bare."	Lockwood	XXXIV

Romantic love and obsession

Quote	Character	Chapter
"He got on to the bed, and wrenched open the lattice, bursting, as he pulled at it, into an uncontrollable passion of tears.'Come in! come in!' [...] Oh! my heart's darling!'"	Lockwood (about Heathcliff)	III
"I love him: and that, not because he's handsome, Nelly, but because he's more myself than I am. Whatever our souls are made of, his and mine are the same"	Catherine	IX
"Every Linton on the face of the earth might melt into nothing before I could consent to forsake Heathcliff."	Catherine	IX
"If all else perished, and he remained, I should still continue to be; and if all else remained, and he were annihilated, the universe would turn to a mighty stranger: I should not seem a part of it."	Catherine	IX
"My love for Linton is like the foliage in the woods: time will change it, I'm well aware, as winter changes the trees. My love for Heathcliff resembles the eternal rocks beneath: a source of little visible delight, but necessary."	Catherine	IX
"I've fought through a bitter life since I last heard your voice; [...] I struggled only for you!"	Heathcliff	X
"The stab of a knife could not inflict a worse pang than [Edgar] suffered at seeing his lady vexed."	Nelly	X

"I have such faith in Linton's love, that I believe I might kill him, and he wouldn't wish to retaliate"	Catherine	X
"I have a right to kiss her, if she chooses; and you have no right to object. I am not *your* husband: *you* needn't be jealous of me!"	Heathcliff	XI
"Will you give up Heathcliff hereafter, or will you give up me? It is impossible for you to be my friend and his at the same time"	Edgar	XI
"For every thought she spends on Linton she spends a thousand on me!"	Heathcliff	XIV
"If he loved with all the powers of his puny being, he couldn't love as much in eighty years as I could in a day."	Heathcliff	XIV
"Two words would comprehend my future – *death* and *hell:* existence, after losing her, would be hell."	Heathcliff	XIV
"Because misery and degradation, and death, and nothing that God or Satan could inflict would have parted us, *you,* of your own will, did it."	Heathcliff	XV
"Be with me always – take any form – drive me mad! only *do* not leave me in this abyss, where I cannot find you! [...] I *cannot* live without my life! I *cannot* live without my soul!"	Heathcliff	XVI
"I went and opened one of the windows; moved by his perseverance to give him a chance of bestowing on the faded image of his idol one final adieu."	Nelly	XVI
"I cannot look down to this floor, but her features are shaped in the flags! In every cloud, in every tree – [...] I am surrounded with her image!"	Heathcliff	XXXIII
"The entire world is a dreadful collection of memoranda that she did exist, and that I have lost her!"	Heathcliff	XXXIII

Social class and race

Quote	Character	Chapter
"He is a dark-skinned gipsy in aspect, in dress and manners a gentleman"	Lockwood (about Heathcliff)	I
"I began to doubt whether he were a servant or not: his dress and speech were both rude [...] and his hands were embrowned like those of a common labourer: still his bearing was free, almost haughty"	Lockwood (about Hareton)	II
"Mrs. Earnshaw was ready to fling it out of doors: she did fly up, asking how he could fashion to bring that gipsy brat into the house"	Nelly	IV
"And Hareton has been cast out like an unfledged dunnock! The unfortunate lad is the only one in all this parish that does not guess how he has been cheated."	Nelly	IV
"I declare he is that strange acquisition my late neighbour made, in his journey to Liverpool – a little Lascar, or an American or Spanish castaway." "A wicked boy, at all events [...] and quite unfit for a decent house!"	Old Mr & Mrs Linton	VI
"I must wish for Edgar Linton's great blue eyes and even forehead [...] I do – and that won't help me to them."	Heathcliff	VII
"You're fit for a prince in disguise. Who knows but your father was Emperor of China, and your mother an Indian queen. [...] Were I in your place, I would frame high notions of my birth"	Nelly (to Heathcliff)	VII
"I wish I had light hair and a fair skin, and was dressed and behaved as well, and had a chance of being as rich as he will be!"	Heathcliff	VII
"Did it never strike you that if Heathcliff and I married, we should be beggars?"	Catherine	IX
"He will be rich, and I shall like to be the greatest woman of the neighbourhood, and I shall be proud of having such a husband."	Catherine	IX
"You will escape from a disorderly, comfortless home into a wealthy, respectable one"	Nelly	IX

Quote	Character	Chapter
"It would degrade me to marry Heathcliff now"	Catherine	IX
"The whole household need not witness the sight of your welcoming a runaway servant as a brother."	Edgar	X
"Papa is gone to fetch my cousin from London: my cousin is a gentleman's son."	Cathy	XVIII
"Mustn't he be made to do as I ask him?"	Cathy	XVIII
"I've got him faster than his scoundrel of a father secured me, and lower; for he takes a pride in his brutishness."	Heathcliff	XXI
"He imagined himself to be as accomplished as Linton, I suppose, because he could spell his own name; and was marvellously discomfited that I didn't think the same."	Cathy	XXIV
"Heathcliff has claimed and kept them in his wife's right and his also: I suppose legally; at any rate, Catherine, destitute of cash and friends, cannot disturb his possession."	Zillah	XXX

Vengeance and retribution

Quote	Character	Chapter
"I'm trying to settle how I shall pay Hindley back. I don't care how long I wait, if I can only do it at last."	Heathcliff	VII
"It is for God to punish wicked people; we should learn to forgive."	Nelly	VII
"Had it been dark, I daresay he would have tried to remedy the mistake by smashing Hareton's skull on the steps"	Nelly	IX
"I felt that God had forsaken the stray sheep there to its own wicked wanderings, and an evil beast prowled between it and the fold, waiting his time to spring and destroy."	Nelly (about Heathcliff)	X
"The tyrant grinds down his slaves and they don't turn against him; they crush those beneath them. You are welcome to torture me to death for your amusement, only allow me to amuse myself a little in the same style"	Heathcliff	XI

Quote	Character	Chapter
"You have treated me infernally [...] and if you fancy I'll suffer unrevenged, I'll convince you of the contrary"	Heathcliff	XI
"Well, if I cannot keep Heathcliff for my friend – if Edgar will be mean and jealous, I'll try to break their hearts by breaking my own. That will be a prompt way of finishing all"	Catherine	XI
"You teach me how cruel you've been – cruel and false. *Why* do you despise me? [...] You deserve this. You have killed yourself."	Heathcliff	XV
"I may take an eye for an eye, a tooth for a tooth; for every wrench of agony return a wrench: reduce him to my level."	Isabella	XVII
"Besides he's *mine,* and I want the triumph of seeing *my* descendant fairly lord of their estates: my child hiring their children to till their father's land for wages."	Heathcliff (about Linton's inheritance)	XX
"Miss Cathy [. . .] was amazed at the blackness of spirit that could brood on and cover revenge for years, and deliberately prosecute its plans without a visitation of remorse."	Nelly	XXI
"Mr. Heathcliff, *you* have *nobody* to love you; and, however miserable you make us, we shall still have the revenge of thinking that your cruelty arises from your greater misery."	Cathy	XXIX
"My old enemies have not beaten me; now would be the precise time to revenge myself on their representatives: I could do it; and none could hinder me. But where is the use? [...] I have lost the faculty of enjoying their destruction, and I am too idle to destroy for nothing."	Heathcliff	XXXIII

Supernatural

Quote	Character	Chapter
"I've progressed in the Black Art: I shall soon be competent to make a clear house of it. The red cow didn't die by chance; and your rheumatism can hardly be reckoned among providential visitations!"	Cathy (in argument with Joseph)	II
"I muttered, knocking my knuckles through the glass, and stretching an arm out to seize the importunate branch; instead of which, my fingers closed on the fingers of a little, ice-cold hand!"	Lockwood	III
"I discerned, obscurely, a child's face looking through the window. Terror made me cruel; and, finding it useless to attempt shaking the creature off, I pulled its wrist on to the broken pane, and rubbed it to and fro till the blood ran down"	Lockwood	III
"Twenty years. I've been a waif for twenty years!"	Catherine (ghost)	III
"She must have been a changeling – wicked little soul! She told me she had been walking the earth these twenty years: a just punishment for her mortal transgressions, I've no doubt!"	Lockwood	III
"The spectre showed a spectre's ordinary caprice: it gave no sign of being; but the snow and wind whirled wildly through, even reaching my station, and blowing out the light."	Lockwood	III
"The angels were so angry that they flung me out into the middle of the heath on the top of Wuthering Heights; where I woke sobbing for joy."	Catherine	IX
"You said I killed you – haunt me, then! The murdered *do* haunt their murderers, I believe. I know that ghosts *have* wandered on earth."	Heathcliff	XVI
"She has disturbed me, night and day, through eighteen years – incessantly – remorselessly – till yesternight; and yesternight I was tranquil. I dreamt I was sleeping the last sleep by that sleeper, with my heart stopped and my cheek frozen against hers."	Heathcliff	XXIX

Quote	Speaker	Chapter
"You know I was wild after she died; and eternally, from dawn to dawn, praying her to return to me her spirit! I have a strong faith in ghosts: I have a conviction that they can, and do, exist among us!"	Heathcliff	XXIX
"I appeared to feel the warm breath of it displacing the sleet-laden wind. I knew no living thing in flesh and blood was by; but, as certainly as you perceive the approach to some substantial body in the dark, though it cannot be discerned, so certainly I felt that [Catherine] was there"	Heathcliff	XXIX
"Yet that old man by the kitchen fire affirms he has seen two on'em looking out of his chamber window on every rainy night since his death"	Nelly	XXXIV
"There are those who speak to having met him near the church, and on the moor, and even within this house."	Nelly (on Heathcliff's ghost)	XXXIV

Section 8

Sample Essays

Essay 1

QUESTION: To what extent does Emily Brontë use form to convey *Wuthering Heights'* Gothic tone?

ESSAY	COMMENTS
INTRODUCTION In her 1847 novel, *Wuthering Heights,* Emily Brontë[1] employs a variety of unique structural features to present a tale shrouded in mystery and speculation. Brontë's text revolves around Gothic features[2] of strong emotions, odd characters, and most importantly a foreboding uncanny atmosphere. Specifically, she highlights these features through her use of a framed narrative structure, multiple voices, and a dual storyline which leaves the reader to draw conclusions subject to the bias of the narrators.[3] Hence, Brontë skilfully explores a range of Gothic ideas to create an overarching tone of uncertainty using multiple narrative devices, thus using form to significant[4] extent in her text.[5]	1. It's always helpful to introduce the title, author, and publication date at the start of your essay. 2. Since the question has asked us to address 'Gothic tone,' it's a good idea to define your understanding of what makes a Gothic text. Here I've chosen to spotlight the characters, their heightened emotions, and eeriness – I'll refer to these throughout my body paragraphs. 3. Let's clearly signpost what to expect in the body paragraphs. 4. We also want to make clear the degree to which we agree or disagree with the question by quantifying 'extent' – some good words to use include: significant, large, considerable, moderate, some, minimal, etc. 5. This is our thesis sentence.

PARAGRAPH 1

The framed structure[6] of the narrative contributes greatly to the unknown and elusive 'truth' of the story, because the reader is learning from a secondary source. This allows Brontë to delve into the speculative nature of Gothic fiction,[7] where readers are given less-than-concrete truths. Although Lockwood describes Nelly as "a very fair narrator," the reader must exercise caution in this appraisal because Lockwood was never privy to any of Nelly's story firsthand. His judgement of her narration relies heavily on his opinion of her character and, from the early chapters of the text, the reader quickly becomes aware he is not as good a judge of character as he thinks he is. For example, he mistakes Heathcliff for a "capital fellow" despite his brusque and uninviting manner. Lockwood's judgements also tend to be fairly superficial, often commenting on the appearance of other characters and conflating his opinions with his own sense of ego. He judges Cathy a "beneficent fairy"[8] based on her beauty and "with that face, [he is] sure [she] cannot help being good-hearted." By introducing Lockwood's personal opinions into the story, the reader is led to question[9] the knowledge being presented. The presentation of the vast array of characters depends on how both Nelly and Lockwood perceive them, overlaying the tale with mystery[10] and bias.

6. This is my first example of form. In this topic sentence we have signposted our argument, provided evidence of a structural technique employed in *Wuthering Heights,* and restated our degree of agreeance (i.e. 'greatly').

7. It is good to link back to the genre, especially because it's part of the prompt.

8. Notice how I've choosen very short quotes as my evidence for this paragraph. Effective use of succinct and relevant quotes can actually elevate your essay because it shows your confident knowledge of the text and can give you more space to expand upon your ideas. (Plus they're easier to remember!)

9. Outlining how the reader is positioned can also further corroborate your argument.

10. Although we haven't explicitly used the words 'Gothic tone' in our linking sentence, since we have already established what Gothic features are, we can still make implied connections to the prompt by relating our point back to a key Gothic feature – mystery.

PARAGRAPH 2

Additionally, Brontë uses a range of text styles to construct the multifaceted nature of the novel, such as Lockwood's diary-like prose, Nelly's recounts, and Isabella's letter. Each character has different experiences and interactions with others, and the amalgamation of all their stories together is what conveys a Gothic air of uncertainty.[11] For example, based on Lockwood's assessment of Hareton, he is a "clown" and "the consequence of being buried alive," implying that he is unattractive and laughable.[12] However, Nelly's recount of Hareton's birth and upbringing reforms this perspective bestowed on the reader, painting him as her "bonny little nursling" and the "finest lad that ever breathed." Furthermore, Isabella's letter describes him as a "ruffianly child" who threatens to set the dogs on her. The conflicting portrayal of the character piques the reader's interest and causes them to wonder what happened to change Hareton. In Isabella's letter to Nelly, after her marriage to Heathcliff, is used to reveal a sudden change and failing of Isabella's affections for Heathcliff, furthering his Gothic characterisation. Despite her previous infatuation due to his charm she begins to question: "Is Mr Heathcliff a man? If so, is he mad? And if not, is he a devil?" These multiple and contrasting perspectives and text styles form a mysterious backstory and is an example of how Brontë's use of different narrative voices can enhance the Gothic[13] characterisation through the portrayal of the unknown and odd characters.

11. Here we are acknowledging how different parts of the text interact with each other and what it aims to show the reader.

12. Since the meaning of "clown" and "consequence of being buried alive" may not be immediately clear, we can take a few words to explain the quote itself. This simultaneously demonstrates our own understanding as well.

13. Each paragraph essentially links back to the Gothic.

PARAGRAPH 3

Brontë's use of a dual storyline fluctuating between the 18th century and the early 19th century allows her to slowly fill in the gaps in the reader's knowledge, whilst simultaneously maintaining a high sense of uncertainty. This means that the reader can see how actions of the past have directly affected the present, although they may not yet know *how* this came to be. An example of this is Heathcliff's display of emotion through an "uncontrollable passion of tears" as he begged Catherine's ghost to come into Wuthering Heights.[14] This event takes place in 1801, which is the present day when Lockwood is retelling his story. At this point in the novel, Catherine has only been identified through her diary entry and the multiple inscriptions of her name on the ledge, intriguingly accompanied by three different surnames. It is not until Nelly's recount of Heathcliff's outburst following Catherine's death that readers learn why he is desperate for her to haunt him. He beseeches Catherine to "take any form – drive [him] mad! only do not leave me."[15] Brontë's use of ghosts in both storylines furthers solidifies *Wuthering Heights* as a Gothic text. Later in her story, she provides more information about how he unearthed her grave to find "that [Catherine] was there: not under [him], but on the earth." Through Nelly's secondhand recount (the past storyline), the reader is able to understand the reasoning for Heathcliff's obsessive behaviour and strong emotions which characterise his present decline into insanity. Hence, Brontë's use of a dual storyline can keep the reader speculating about the ominous and Gothically supernatural occurrences in the present.[16]

14. Since this paragraph is talking about the dual storyline, I want to make sure I'm using evidence from multiple points across the story. This first quote is from early on in the novel.

15. Here is a quote taken from later on during Catherine's timeline just before her death. Now we have provided two points of relevant evidence.

16. Since this is our third paragraph we can also take the conclusions of the first two and extend upon them. Ideas in essays don't need to be restricted to their own body paragraph (although feel free to disregard if you find a more structured approach easier!). Imagine your essay like a tower of building blocks; with each argument we add, we also add another block and by the conclusion the marker should be able to view your 'tower' as a whole and cohesive piece of writing.

CONCLUSION	
Brontë uses many narrative devices to create an enthralling Gothic tale in which use of a framed narrative and multiple voices allows the reader to gauge the opinions and experiences of a variety of characters. This presents multiple perspectives on the same events and can help explain the strange behaviours and beliefs of other characters. Her use of a dual storyline also enhances the reader's ability to make correlations between the past and present as the story is pieced together, adding to the foreboding sense which characterises Gothic literature.[17] Hence, Brontë uses form to a significant extent, through multiple structural devices and narrative features, to create a text that effectively explores the Gothic concept of the unknown.[18]	17. In the conclusion, provide a brief overview of each paragraph. Remember not to introduce new information. 18. Here we've restated and once more answered the question.

Essay 2

QUESTION: Brontë amalgamates love and destruction in her portrayal of Heathcliff and Catherine's relationship. Discuss.

ESSAY	COMMENTS
INTRODUCTION [1] Love and destruction may appear mutually exclusive; however, love in the form of obsession[2] can easily become destructive. Emily Brontë's 1847 novel *Wuthering Heights* explores the way love can morph into an obsession, which ultimately damaged Heathcliff and Catherine's relationships and led to their destruction. In this way, the text examines the role obsession plays in destroying the goodness and humanity of love, becoming detrimental to a person's health and wellbeing. Throughout her novel, Brontë ties these concepts back to the Gothic genre, wherein overpowering emotions often pave the way for the downfall of important characters.[3] By portraying Catherine and Heathcliff's journey of love, obsession, and destruction, Brontë shows the reader that all-consuming feelings can ruin relationships and lives, leading to devastation.[4]	1. Before we even start planning or writing the essay we need to understand the prompt. It can help to underline key or difficult words such as amalgamate (which means to fuse or unite into one). Although we are not explicitly being asked a question, we still want to take a clear stance in our response which we can do by agreeing or disagreeing. 2. I chose to take a more nuanced approach to a question. Love and destruction can take many forms and as such you can explore more complex ideas, but here I wanted to focus on how obsessive love can become destructive. 3. Here's a link back to genre – this is pertinent because big emotions like love are a major feature of the Gothic genre. 4. This is the thesis. It is slightly more complex than the previous essay as we have multiple parts to address: the characters and their portrayal, love and destruction, and what we're discussing.

PARAGRAPH 1

Heathcliff and Catherine's love in *Wuthering Heights* becomes synonymous with destruction, not just for their relationships with those around them. This amalgamation[5] is so quintessential[6] it manifests in the literary canon[7] as a famous example of Gothic love, unbreakable by "misery and degradation, and death." Their innocent connection in childhood is seen early on through Nelly's observation of how their "little souls were comforting each other" following Old Mr Earnshaw's death.[8] However, the love they shared in their younger years quickly becomes a mutual obsession as Heathcliff and Catherine grow up. This obsession wreaks havoc on her marriage with Edgar. She emasculates him after Heathcliff's return, admonishing him for his "weak nature" and tells him to "make an apology, or allow yourself to be beaten." Brontë unveils Catherine's vanity and love for Heathcliff through her indulgence of his violent tendencies. Even in childhood when Heathcliff throws applesauce at Edgar, Catherine reprimands Edgar first for making "mischief" and for having "spoilt" the visit. Catherine's obsession with Heathcliff motivates her to try to keep him in her life, despite the cost to her and Edgar's "deep and growing happiness." Hence, their previously innocent love morphs into an obsession with the destructive power capable of ruining their other relationships.

5. Using keywords from the prompt is a great way to link back to the main ideas of your essay.

6. Here's a quantifier to show the marker my position on the prompt (I agree).

7. By placing the text in the context of the literary canon (a body of classics that are largely considered to be important or majorly influential) I can further support and give a solid basis to my own argument.

8. I haven't launched straight into love/destruction, but instead chosen to provide some context of Catherine and Heathcliff's childhood relationship as this is also a part of Brontë's portrayal of her characters. By showcasing diverse pieces of evidence we can strengthen our overall argument (and there's plenty of space to do so when responding to a 'discussion' question without veering away from your main points).

PARAGRAPH 2

Heathcliff's obsession with Catherine causes irrevocable damage to his own state of mind and Catherine's too.[9] Their love is described using imagery: "the eternal rocks beneath: a source of little visible delight, but necessary," implying that it will always be. A more modern interpretation[10] could connect the "eternal rocks" of this quote the tectonic plates beneath the Earth's surface. They cannot be seen but are an intrinsic part of our planet and can exact powerful forces in the form of natural disaster, much like the destruction of the pair's love. Catherine initiates destruction as she weaponises her health against Heathcliff (and Edgar) when she plans to "break their hearts by breaking [her] own" as a "prompt way of finishing all." On her deathbed, Catherine's love further gives way to anger as she curses Heathcliff: "I wish I could hold you [...] till we were both dead!" The contradiction of her desire to hurt him and comfort him resembles the internal conflict Heathcliff experiences and further displays their love as destructive; he dreads having her words eat "deeper eternally after [she has] left." Brontë's use of highly emotive dialogue further intertwines love and destruction as inherent to their relationship. The strength of their connection is furthered by Catherine's metaphorical statement: "I am *Heathcliff!*" She sees their souls as entwined and can never be separated. While a romantic statement, conjuring notions of idyllic and shared love, there are consequences for their 'joint' "soul"[11] as Catherine spirals into self-destruction.

9. My argument for paragraph two is that their love is destructive to themselves, leading on from paragraph one where we talked about how their love impacted others (specifically Catherine's marriage).

10. Although *Wuthering Heights* was published in 1847, don't be afraid to draw on and discuss ideas from the 21st century.

11. It can be effective to formulate your ideas and explanations using a single important word from a quote. The "soul" is a recurring idea and defines Catherine and Heathcliff's relationship and connection, making it an advantageous inclusion in your essay.

While Catherine self-destructs, Heathcliff's downfall is also catalysed, as he ponders how to live with his "soul in the grave." Hence their mutual obsession has caused both irreversible damage. For Catherine, her destruction is her separation from Heathcliff in death, and for him it is his separation from her in life.[12]

PARAGRAPH 3

The final aspect of their destructive love comes about in the decades leading up to and following Catherine's death; Heathcliff's mental health declines as he frequents her gravesite and wandered the moors in search of her ghost.[13] Heathcliff states: "for every thought she spends on Linton she spends a thousand on me! [...] I had a notion of the kind: it haunted me." Brontë's use of hyperbole[14] in this dialogue reveals the extent of his obsession with Catherine; while viewing her love for him as superior to Edgar's, it is also made clear that Heathcliff is plagued by thoughts of her.[15] His obsession takes a morbid turn as he strikes "one side of [Catherine's] coffin loose" ordering that he be buried beside her with his own coffin struck open, so that they could be together in death. He was disturbed by her ghost "night and day, through eighteen years – incessantly." His declining mental state is further manifested in his dreams of "dissolving with her, and being more happy still." All of these events, taking place over eighteen years, culminate in the complete loss of his sanity in his dying days, wherein all he could think of is Catherine. This all-encompassing obsession costs him his life, losing years chasing after Catherine's ghost. Ultimately, Brontë uses their relationship to show how even something as sweet as love can evolve into a self-destructive obsession to the detriment of a person's life.

12. This linking sentence adds another level of complexity to the essay, as destruction doesn't come in one specific form.

13. Finally, let's explore 'destruction' as Heathcliff's downfall whic revolves around the persistence of his love without the presence of its object.

14. Here I've named a literary device.

15. In this sentence, I'm further explaining the characteristics of an obsession.

CONCLUSION

Brontë presents a story of transformation from innocent love to dark obsession that leads to the destruction of multiple parties. She shows that although love itself is a beautiful phenomenon, it can descend into jealousy and demolition, allowing people to lose themselves in their quest to possess the object of their desire. In *Wuthering Heights*, Catherine's[16] obsession with Heathcliff causes her to damage her relationship with her husband and fall into terminal illness. Similarly, Heathcliff's obsession with Catherine becomes an all-consuming fixation and his grief eventually destroys his sanity.[17] Through the caustic nature of Catherine and Heathcliff's obsessive relationship, Brontë merges love and destruction to show how deeply humans are affected by their emotions.[18]

16. Since the prompt is very specific about which characters it wants us to discuss, make sure you continue to bring your discussion back to Catherine and Heathcliff.

17. Sometimes you can recap the essay body in one sentence, but it's also fine to restate your points over multiple sentences.

18. Let's reiterate our thesis with slightly more nuance. I've called the nature of their relationship 'caustic' – a word with *destructive* connotations as caustic substances can burn or be corrosive.

Essay 3

QUESTION: Compare and contrast how the need for vengeance leads to the corruption of love in Emily Brontë's *Wuthering Heights*.

ESSAY	COMMENTS
INTRODUCTION [1]The human desire for retribution can corrupt even the purest forms of love as it taints affection with a need for destruction. Emily Brontë's 1847 novel *Wuthering Heights* explores how vengeance can corrupt love through the characterisation of Heathcliff, Catherine, and Edgar. Distinctively, Heathcliff's vendetta against the Earnshaw family causes a rift that corrupts his love for Catherine, transforming it into a painful affair that carries on long after her death. Brontë depicts him as a damaged and vengeful Byronic hero,[2] elucidating how his contempt for the Lintons and Earnshaws impedes his love for Catherine. Similarly, Catherine's love for him clashes with her need to hurt him, ultimately taking her life. By contrast, Edgar is one of the few characters disinterested in revenge, and Brontë shows how avoidance of retaliation can influence love positively.[3] Hence, Brontë reveals not only how vengeance has the power to corrupt love, but how renouncing revenge can constructively benefit relationships.[4]	1. Like the previous essay, this essay prompt also mentions love but let's notice how they are different. We've now got a focus on 'vengeance,' so we can start identifying multiple characters who want payback to use their quotes as evidence. Additionally, we are asked to 'compare and contrast,' so when constructing your arguments be prepared to present cases of similarities and differences. 2. Touching on prominent character archtypes can provide helpful background information and inform your arguments (much like talking about genre). 3. I've chosen two characters which show how vengences corrupts (Heathcliff and Catherine) so I can 'compare' them, and another character adverse to vengence (Edgar) to 'contrast' my other examples. 4. Here's my thesis statement.

PARAGRAPH 1

Humans have an inherent desire to feel loved and accepted by those they value; however, they also crave retribution for the wrongs that have been done against them. In *Wuthering Heights,* Heathcliff faces a significant conflict between his need for Catherine's love and his vow to see her family destroyed as a punishment for his past sufferings, leading to the corruption of his love.[5] On one hand, he is certain that there is no force in the universe that can overcome their love, claiming that "misery and degradation, and death, and nothing that God or Satan could inflict" could separate them. However, his use of the word *degrade* in this statement may be an allusion to the contempt he felt when Catherine said it would "degrade [her] to marry [him]." He holds this rejection against her for the rest of her life, marring their love with his perceived burden of inferiority to Edgar in class, wealth, status, and Catherine's preference. Brontë uses this growing hurt as an avenue to explore the development of Heathcliff's character as he starts to lose himself to his vengeance. He embodies the characteristics of a Byronic hero,[6] experiencing intense negative emotions[7] and devoting his life to the destruction of others. She presents the readers with a character arc that slowly strays away from a romantic hero, and ventures into the territory of a villainous antihero. By allowing his vengeance to control his life and spoil his relationship with Catherine, Brontë reveals how revenge can corrupt love.

5. This sentence highlights a clear dissonance between Heathcliff's two main desires.

6. Again talking about the Byronic hero archetype is suitable here because they often seek revenge.

7. A subtle link to feature that appears in Gothic literature.

PARAGRAPH 2

Catherine is also characterised by her vanity and need for petty revenge;[8] she distorts her love for others using manipulation. She starves herself and exacerbates her illness seemingly to spite Heathcliff and Edgar. When she is on her deathbed, she causes Heathcliff anguish aiming to deliberately upset him: "you have killed me – and thriven on it." Through his response, Heathcliff paints their separation as Catherine's own fault, saying "you have killed yourself. [...] You loved me – then what right had you to leave me?" His rhetorical question draws attention to the idea that she abandoned her love for him in search of material pleasure, and that now she takes solace in saying words that will haunt him once she is dead. Brontë characterises Catherine as headstrong in pursuit of her ideals, but plagued by her own selfishness.[9] Her need to "break [Heathcliff and Edgar's] hearts by breaking [her] own" reveals that she needs to achieve the satisfaction of knowing both men will be haunted by her death, even if that means forsaking the purity of her love. Catherine's vengeance manifests as a desire to be remembered and a need to hurt others as a method of control, which Brontë implies ultimately tarnishes her love for others.[10]

8. Here we have pinpointed that Catherine is similar to Heathcliff (as a means of comparison), but by labelling her revenge as 'petty' we have also draw attention to the difference between her and Heathcliff's revenge based on 'inferiority.'

9. Here we have identified 'selfishness' as a corruptor and motive.

10. Let's make a strong link to thesis, accompanied by a direct analysis of Catherine to refine and link our point.

PARAGRAPH 3

In contrast to Heathcliff and Catherine, Edgar is disinclined to pursue revenge; thus, Brontë positions him as selfless and having an incorruptible love for his wife and daughter. In the first arc of the narrative, Edgar often acquiesces to Catherine's wants to please her. Although Brontë seems to mock[11] Edgar's love for Catherine – he is as powerless "to depart as [...] a cat possesses the power to leave a mouse half killed, or a bird half eaten" – she also praises his selfless love for her. He lavishes on her "kindest caresses" and "fondest words" while she is ill despite her continued association with Heathcliff and stays with her until death, watching over her corpse like a silent "guardian." He does not seek revenge[12] for the part Heathcliff plays in Catherine's death or for his elopement with Isabella, but merely "avoid[s] his house and family" encouraging his daughter to do the same. When Cathy discovers Wuthering Heights and Linton's true residence there, he dissuades her from visiting but eventually relents, letting her meet with her cousin and foster a relationship. Despite the risk of his assets falling into Heathcliff's hands, he considers the prospect of Cathy's marriage to Linton, prioritising her happiness above all. Overall, Brontë portrays Edgar in an admirable light, with his love, loyalty, and hope in his relationships uncorrupted by the need for revenge.

11. Again, it might seem a little unconventional to insert multiple interpretations of the text, but if done well, this can add depth to your discussion. Just make sure you don't 'fence-sit' by introducing a bunch of conflicting interpretations that you can't resolve into an overall thesis. Here we aim to convey that Edgar's disinclination for revenge is even more admirable when we account for the mockery and insults he has endured.

12. Make your arguments are clear as possible. We might already know that Edgar isn't portrayed as vengeful, but make sure to explicitly tell the marker that!

CONCLUSION

Brontë uses well-constructed Gothic characters of Heathcliff and Catherine to reveal an innate but destructive propensity for vengeance, even in the face of intense love. Heathcliff's lifelong goal to inflict pain upon the Earnshaws and Lintons corrupts his love for Catherine, embodying the archetype of the Byronic hero as he embraces his violent desperation for retribution. In turn, Catherine's characterisation as a stubborn and wild heroine allows Brontë to show how her vanity, manipulation, and need to be remembered tarnish her love. In contrast[13] to these two characters, Edgar's love remains incorruptible. His aversion to violence and narcissism, which characterises Heathcliff and Catherine, starkly opposes the vengeance they both succumb to.[14] Ultimately, Brontë privileges that revenge yields unattainable satisfaction and only functions to detriment self, relationships, and love.[15]

13. Here's a clear signpost showing I've addressed the prompt.
14. I like to include an overview of my body paragraphs in every essay.
15. Conclusions can sometimes be hard to write when you feel you've already said all you've needed to say in the body paragraphs, but don't be afraid to repeat and reiterate! Here we've closed with a reiteration of our thesis.

Essay 4

QUESTION: How does Brontë use the supernatural to explore the afterlife, death, and grief in *Wuthering Heights?*

ESSAY	COMMENTS
INTRODUCTION The presence of the supernatural in Gothic literature alludes to the close relationship characters have with death, and how aspects of this connection to the afterlife seep into their daily lives. In Brontë's 1847 novel *Wuthering Heights,* death is an ever-present theme that haunts almost every character through grief, and the use of supernatural forces only amplifies this feeling of loss.[1] Heathcliff and Catherine's supernatural connection to the afterlife is represented through their inexplicable metaphysical bond, and the motif of ghosts throughout the story. The special link between the two characters transcends the barrier of death, allowing the reader to question its permanence and existence after death. To provide a Gothic manifestation of this bond, Brontë uses ghosts as comment on death, the afterlife and the impermanence of life, but also on the loss and grief present in *Wuthering Heights.*[2]	1. This is a 'how' question so make sure you use plenty of descriptors to support your arguments. Think about how techniques are used. What has the author done on purpose? Do their context, genre, or themes affect their portrayal of ideas? Here we've said the supernatural has been used to 'amplify' other ideas. 2. Here's our thesis touching on ghosts (the primary supernatural element of *Wuthering Heights*), as well as keywords from the prompt (life, death, and grief).

PARAGRAPH 1

From a young age, both Catherine and Heathcliff find themselves surrounded by death, which aids the foundations of their relationship with the supernatural through grief. Both Old Mr and Mrs Earnshaw pass away while the characters are children, and before long, even Frances, the new mistress of Wuthering Heights is gone. Nelly presents the reader with their first proper encounter with death as deepening their bond,[3] as their "little souls were comforting each other." She explains that "no parson in the world ever pictured heaven so beautifully as they did, in their innocent talk," revealing how both children connected with each other over the shared experience of death by picturing an afterlife in heaven. Such a harrowing experience plays a significant role in their everyday lives as they struggled to adjust to their new environment; however, it also served to strengthen their relationship. Even when Hindley returns and puts Heathcliff to work, Catherine "taught him what she learnt, and worked or played with him in the fields." This shows how Brontë uses their perception of death and the afterlife to complement the development of Heathcliff and Catherine's supernatural bond.

3. This links death to the supernatural bond between the characters, establishing the relationship Gothic characters have with life and the afterlife.

PARAGRAPH 2

Brontë uses the supernatural to challenge the inevitable separation of death. This is demonstrated after Catherine's passing, when Heathcliff continues to connect with her despite the lack of her physical presence.[4] Following her death, he digs up her grave, longing to see her one more time. Her ghost becomes a physical manifestation of his grief as he feels her presence beside him, hearing "a sigh from some one above, close at the edge of the grave." Since that day, he explains that "she has disturbed [him], night and day, through eighteen years," haunting him and driving his desperation to see her. He has dreams of death and chasing her fleeting presence out into the cold of the moor in the dead of night, reinforcing the idea of their bond transcending death. The supernatural occurrence of Heathcliff sensing Catherine's ghost around him time and time again reveals the deep connection he has to the afterlife and death itself but also the all-consuming nature of his grief.[5] Thus, using supernatural forces such as ghosts and an intangible bond, Brontë explores the relationship between Gothic characters and what lies beyond the veil.

4. This clearly reflects our main idea that death is normal to the characters and does not hinder their relationship.

5. As Heathcliff regularly experiences ghostly apparitions, it shows that his relationship with Catherine and the afterlife is extremely strong.

PARAGRAPH 3

Furthermore, in Heathcliff's final days he isolates himself from the living world, opting to spend his time with Catherine's ghost. He also has an uncanny knowledge of his own death,[6] stating: "I am within sight of my heaven. I have my eyes on it: hardly three feet to sever me!" This unusual understanding of his own impending passing links to the supernatural ideals Brontë has embedded in the text, wherein Heathcliff has spent his whole life surrounded by death. The night before his death, Nelly recalls him speaking to Catherine, "as one would speak to a person present; low and earnest, and wrung from the depth of his soul." Brontë portrays him as having finally caught up to Catherine's elusive ghost in his final hours as he approaches death, signifying his transition from one world to the next.[7] Using his supernatural bond with Catherine and his close connection to death, Brontë also comments on Heathcliff's response to loss as weighing on his health and his sense of mortality.

6. As a Gothic character, we can expect Heathcliff's connection to death and the afterlife is very strong.

7. The lines between the worlds blur for Heathcliff – another Gothic trope.

CONCLUSION

Thus, Brontë explores the connection between the supernatural and death and the afterlife through both Heathcliff and Catherine's grief and reaction to loss. The relationship between the two characters, and its ability to persist even after Catherine's death, reflects the substantial strength of their supernatural bond. Furthermore, through the depiction of ghosts, Brontë is able to amplify Heathcliff's personal connection to Catherine, as well as his knowledge of death. By combining all these aspects of the supernatural in *Wuthering Heights*, Brontë reveals that Gothic characters have deep connections to the supernatural through death and the afterlife, and that this becomes a part of who they are.[8]

8. Again, where possible, try to decant all the points you've discussed throughout your essay into an even more nuanced take on your thesis – it will really cement your understanding of the text for the marker.